SPIRITUAL WRITERS
OF THE EARLY CHURCH

IS VOLUME

39

OF THE

Twentieth Century Encyclopedia of Catholicism

UNDER SECTION

IV

THE MEANS OF REDEMPTION

IT IS ALSO THE

10TH

VOLUME IN ORDER OF PUBLICATION

Edited by HENRI DANIEL-ROPS of the Académie Française

SPIRITUAL WRITERS
OF THE EARLY CHURCH

By F. CAYRÉ

Translated from the French by W. WEBSTER WILSON

HAWTHORN BOOKS · PUBLISHERS · *New York*

First Edition, January, 1959

NIHIL OBSTAT

Carolus Davis, S.T.L.

Censor Deputatus

IMPRIMATUR

E. Morrogh Bernard

Vicarius Generalis

Westmonasterii, die VI SEPTEMBRIS MCMLVIII

The Library of Congress has catalogued this publication as follows:

Cayré, Fulbert.

Spiritual writers of the early church. Translated from the French by W. Wilson. [1st ed.] New York, Hawthorn Books [1959]

127 p. 21 cm. (The Twentieth century encyclopedia of Catholicism, v. 39. Section 4: The means of redemption)

Translation of Spirituels et mystiques des premiers temps.
Bibliography: p. 127.

1. Mysticism—Early church.   I. Title.   (Series: The Twentieth century encyclopedia of Catholicism, v. 39)

BV5075.C313   281.1   59–6725

CONTENTS

CHAPTER I

THE FIRST WITNESSES OF THE SPIRIT IN THE CHURCH

THE TRUE WITNESSES OF THE HOLY SPIRIT

By these we mean particularly the "Fathers of the Church". We must be careful to distinguish them from the Apostles without, of course, forgetting the many and important points of contact between them.

The Apostles are essentially "witnesses of the living God". St Peter, in the Upper Room, wishing to replace the traitor Judas and complete the symbolic number of the Twelve laid down the primary condition that a candidate for the title of Apostle should have known Jesus Christ personally: "Let him," said the chief of the Twelve, "be one of those men who have walked. in our company all through the time when the Lord Jesus came and went among us, from the time when John used to baptize to the day when he, Jesus, was taken from us" (Acts 1. 21–2). This title is one of unique splendour. The Twelve enjoyed the incomparable privilege of living in intimate contact with the Man-God, as no other human being has done, with the exception of Mary. There is even a sense in which their privilege surpassed hers, for they heard words never uttered before her, even if their substance was previously communicated to her by him in a sublime spiritual manner. He performed before them those actions by which the great mysteries of the Trinity, the Incarnation and the Redemption were to be transmitted to all humanity. Through the Twelve alone God has revealed himself to the world and their witness alone has official value.

St Paul, it is true, did not see Christ on earth, and yet he possesses in a high degree the title of Apostle, since he is associated with St Peter in the cultus rendered to him for centuries by the Church. But it was precisely because he too was a witness of the Man-God, firstly in the very fact of his conversion, when Christ, striking him to the ground, revealed himself in person: "I am Jesus whom Saul persecutes" (Acts 9. 5); and later, in the revelations which he received from Christ, for he boasts of several in his Epistles, and the Acts mention various supernatural favours which make the convert of Damascus a true witness of God. If he did not see Christ in his earthly state he saw him spiritually in his glory, and on this ground he is considered an Apostle. Other disciples, apart from the "Twelve", have also been called Apostles in so far as they too, in a general way, had known our Saviour and could bear witness to his activity, but instances of this are rare. The *Didache* also mentions travelling missionaries, called apostles, who do not seem necessarily to have been eye-witnesses of Christ; but their importance is negligible and they have no place in the apostolic hierarchy. Only the official witnesses gathered together by Christ during his lifetime or shortly after his resurrection are truly Apostles, and their direct influence is maintained until the end of the same century in the person of St John.

At this point the patristic period begins, with the first Christian writers, several of whom knew St John, if not St Peter, and we see in them another essential characteristic, namely, that of *witnesses of the Holy Spirit* in the Church. At his ascension into heaven, Christ told the Apostles that he would soon keep his promise of sending them another like himself, a comforter, a guide, an advocate. This promise was kept and the day of Pentecost, probably in the year 30, saw the inauguration of this new phase in the history of God's Covenant; this was the foundation of the Church by the action of the Holy Spirit. Here the Apostles were not only spectators, but instruments also. So that, having been witnesses of God Incarnate, they now became the "witnesses of the Spirit" acting in the Church. Privileged instruments of grace, they carried out this double mission until their deaths which, according to tradition, sealed it with their blood.

It was this second witness of the Apostles which, at a later date, was specially the rôle of the Fathers, since none of them had seen Christ in person; on this particular question of the action of the Holy Spirit in the Church, however, our Saviour's first disciples supply abundant information, and we must refer to this in its broad outlines, for it was to become the principal source of Christian piety from the earliest times. Of course, these themes are to be found in all the apostolic writings, but those of St Paul and St John are particularly rich in this respect and it is possible to speak of the mysticism of these two Apostles, by grouping together those passages from their works from which it is derived or in which it is clearly shown.

THE APOSTLES, PRECURSORS OF THE FATHERS

The essence of Christianity is a mutual gift of God to man and of man to God, by the action of the Holy Spirit. It is the very life of God brought to humanity by the Word made flesh: "But all those who did welcome him he empowered to become the children of God, all those who believe in his name, their birth came, not from human stock, not from nature's will or man's but from God." St John wrot: these words towards the end of the first century; in them he summed up not only the memory of his own intimate contact with Jesus Christ, which lasted three years, but also that of three-quarters of a century spent in those Christian societies in the east, in Syria and in Asia Minor, which were clearly marked by the thought of St Paul. He himself was in some sort the personification of that thought, and the Fathers received it from his hands as a sacred heritage.

The earliest Christian writings show their author's concern

to give prominence to the Holy Spirit. Even the synoptic Gospels, whose particular function is simply to recall for the benefit of the Christians who still lived in the Pentecostal atmosphere, the earthly life of our Saviour, and particularly his public actions, do not omit this loftier aspect. In two of them it dominates the "Sermon on the Mount", in the beatitudes, which the Fathers were to regard as a peculiar manifestation of the Holy Spirit. St John lays even greater emphasis on it, especially in the words of Christ after the Last Supper: here all is subordinated to the promise of the Spirit whose coming demands the sacrifice of Christ and his departure to heaven: this is the price of Pentecost.

The Epistles repeat the teaching of the Gospels. According to the Acts, St Peter is the first official witness of this action of the Spirit, at the very moment when he begins his public mission, at Pentecost. Peter quotes the prophecy of Joel, but his words recall others, no less illustrious. He himself is to be the highest placed of these ministers of the Holy Spirit in the first days of Christianity, and we cannot fail to be moved on finding restrained but firm mention of it in his Epistles, as in his spoken words. In his second Epistle, he connects this action of the Holy Spirit with his stirring recollection of the Transfiguration, and this reference to it demonstrates its importance in his eyes: "It was never man's impulse, after all, that gave us prophecy; men gave it utterance, but they were men whom God had sanctified, carried away, as they spoke, by the Holy Spirit."

St Paul, more than anyone, lays emphasis on this teaching. It is true that he insisted strongly on the ravages of original sin, notably in the Epistle to the Romans, chs. 5–7. But these passages are usually taken in too great isolation from those in chapter 8, which contains a splendid homage to the action of the Spirit in the baptized. Not only, he declares, is sin destroyed, but in the Christian a new life is established wherein heavenly favours are bestowed, to the extent of intimacy with God, even in this life (5. 12–27), and so is ensured a life of happiness in eternity. These pages on the theological virtues are an echo of the magnificent eulogy pronounced by the Apostle in their honour the previous year, in his first letter to the Corinthians, 13. 1–13.

Every Christian should keep these passages constantly before him; they were the very marrow of the directives given by the Apostle regarding the action of the Holy Spirit in the communities. It is he who gives to the baptized the strength required to struggle against the flesh and its appetites; it is through him that, by degrees, love becomes a force transforming the Law, in proportion as a man learns to submit to it. Then, obedience to the commandment comes less from without than from within, thanks to the Holy Spirit who is given to us. And this outpouring of the Spirit means also sharing in a high degree in the divine life itself, this life which is possessed in its fullness by the Father, the Son and the Holy Spirit. This is the doctrine which, for centuries, was to be the basis of patristic teaching.

The Epistles of St John, particularly the first, bring out the full meaning of the texts in his Gospel referring to the Holy Spirit, here given the name of Unction, to emphasize his connections with him who is the "Anointed One" par excellence, the Christ. Three times, St John gives him this title (2. 20 and 22). This instance is employed to emphasize both the truth which comes from Christ and the charity which is the Apostle's keynote, charity towards one's neighbour as towards God. But the accent is clearly placed on the divine origin of the teaching which powerfully penetrates mind and heart: "Meanwhile, the influence of his anointing lives on in you, so that you have no need of teaching; no lesson his influence gives you can be a lie, they are all true" (2. 27).

THE CENTRAL THEME OF THE WRITINGS OF THE FATHERS

This indeed is the very keynote of the patristic writings; the early Christian writings introduce us into a region saturated with divine life, the fruit of baptism, and enlivened by the action of the Holy Spirit, in whom Christ continues to rule the

Church. In reality, the Fathers are the first mystics of Christendom. In our time this aspect of their character is too often forgotten. We think of them primarily as witnesses of faith, as ardent apologists and controversialists, even as founders of schools in the modern sense of the word, and thus we run the risk of distorting their true character by laying insufficient emphasis on something which is essential to it, namely supernatural life.

This supernatural life is truly fundamental to their works, and it is this which must be given especial prominence. There is no question of neglecting faith, but it must not be separated from that charity which is its very soul, as St Paul says when he reminds the Galatians that "once we are in Christ, circumcision means nothing, and the want of it means nothing; the faith that finds its expression in love is all that matters" (Gal. 5. 6).

This elementary truth is admitted in principle by all members of the Church. But, in practice, it is rarely given the importance due to it even by those writing of ancient times, and all the more so when we come to more recent periods. It too often happens that the Church is contemplated under various aspects taken separately, which prevents any profound vision of the whole, except in the case of those who are especially drawn to it. It is precisely this weakness which we would wish to remedy by presenting some essential ancient texts dealing with the subject.

The gifts of the Holy Spirit may be regarded as the central theme, for the Fathers themselves have given numerous descriptions of them. They present them as a higher divine force giving life to all genuine Christianity and imbuing it with intense vitality, from every point of view, in the field of doctrine as in that of action. For them, normally these two aspects are indissolubly united; this is one of the outstanding features of the primitive Church, and it remained so for centuries. It is perhaps the most noticeable characteristic of the patristic period.

Thus there is a great deal to be gained by bringing this

teaching to light, not regarding it simply from a theoretical or literary viewpoint, but situating it in the living framework of ancient times, whether of Christendom in general or of the Christian soul responding generously to the promptings of grace, for it is in grace alone that we must seek the true spiritual life.

Of course, numerous centres of fervent spiritual activity are to be found in antiquity, even outside the cloister, and by seeking along these lines it is possible to find valuable indications touching the deep life of the primitive Christian societies. Even doctrinal works have a spiritual tone which is an echo of their environment, and this is still truer in the case of sermons or religious treatises. We can draw real enlightenment from them if we are prepared to find it.

We shall confine ourselves here to noting the richest sources dealing with this special theme of the gifts of the Holy Spirit, furnished by the list drawn up by Isaias in reference to the expected Messias. Not that we are restricted to this brief document, but it serves to group together a number of patristic texts which, precisely, are concerned with the very highest aspects of the spiritual life. Herein lies their importance. Long before Christ, the Spirit of God is mentioned in the Old Testament as being the source of illumination, moral or intellectual, prophetic or artistic. With the Psalms and the Sapiential books, the religious and moral note comes to the fore and becomes dominant in fervent religious groups shortly before the coming of Christ.

The text in Isaias plays an extremely important but not exclusive part. About the year 50 B.C., one of the psalms allegedly by Solomon (17. 5) reproduces more or less Isaias' list, the text of which is well known: "From the stock of Jesse a scion shall burgeon yet: out of his roots a flower shall spring. One shall be born, on whom the spirit of the Lord shall rest; a spirit wise and discerning, a spirit prudent and strong, a spirit of knowledge and of piety [fear][1] and ever the fear of the Lord shall fill his heart" (Isaias 11. 1–2).

[1] The word "fear" occurs twice in the Hebrew text. [*Trans.*]

Even if the word *fear*, employed with so many shades of meaning in Scripture, expressed nothing new by its repetition here, the mere fact that it is repeated at the end denotes the figure seven, implying completeness, and that is what we must remember here. The whole Christian tradition, founded on the many septenaries of the Apocalypse (1 and 5), was to interpret it in this sense with a unanimity which has the force of law.

SOURCES OF TEACHING ON THE HOLY SPIRIT

These texts from the Old Testament were given especial emphasis by the Fathers, principally owing to St Paul and St John, whose influence was paramount from the first centuries onwards. Moreover, these two Apostles, in spite of their fundamental agreement, represent many shades of thought which it is as well to emphasize for we find them recurring in the Fathers according to each one's particular gifts and special mission in the Church. The insistence on Christ, in St Paul as in St John, must not make us forget that both assign an important place to the Holy Spirit in the exhortations addressed to the faithful in their Epistles.

St Paul, like St John, proclaimed the teaching of the universal action of the Holy Spirit in all Christians, preparing in advance the diffusion of this doctrine among the Fathers. It became universal, even in the form of the septenarium, the usual form in which it is expressed. St John does not speak of the seven gifts, but he uses the number seven frequently in the Apocalypse, when he talks of the seven Churches, the seven candlesticks, the seven stars, the seven spirits of God, and later he connects his mysterious prophecies with seven seals, seven trumpets, seven signs and seven cups, on each occasion evoking the seven gifts enumerated by Isaias; very quickly the links between them were established. By retaining the figure seven for the actions of the Holy Spirit, Augustine was only consolidating a rule which, for some centuries already, had inspired religious literature, and the divine origin of which was regarded as unquestionable.

"Spiritual Writers and Mystics of the Early Centuries": this title might be taken in a narrow sense to denote a selection from among the ancient writers of the Church. By doing so, however, we should be introducing into Christian antiquity a mental category quite unknown to it. We should run the risk of narrowing down this vast subject and, perhaps, cutting it off from the true sources of its inspiration. In point of fact, all the ancient writers of the Church, in the eight hundred years from the last decades of the first century to the middle of the ninth, may be regarded as "spiritual writers" and "mystics", if we use these words in a broad sense, and this meaning of the word is fully in accordance with the term "Fathers" which the ancient world applied to them from the fifth century onwards, and which still remains in use. It has been progressively extended to writers of the seventh century, to those of the eighth and even to those of the first part of the ninth; but that is the extreme limit.

In actual fact the name Fathers, taken in itself, corresponds very well with a certain spiritual function, and it denotes the appointed instruments of the Holy Spirit in the Mystical Body of Christ. The word can be traced back to the origins of the Church, although it came into general use only as a result of the great Councils, which felt the need of demonstrating the conformity of the new formulas of faith to traditional teaching, especially on the divinity of Christ and his humanity. The term also denoted the authority of these same men in everything appertaining to the rules of the Christian life, particularly the most sublime of them, for at that time no distinction was made between these two aspects of a living reality.

Among these rules, closely bound up with dogmatic belief, but life-giving in their application, those concerning the personal union of souls with God stand out astonishingly from the second century onwards, and still more so in the third and fourth centuries. Wisdom is the outstanding feature and, already, it implied a real intimacy with God, the fruit of lofty knowledge and ardent love, both attributed to a higher action of grace. All the great Doctors benefited by it; but the most eminent of them, in this sphere as in many others, is St Augustine, and through him we hear the voice not only of the ancient Church of the west, but that of the east too, for he was acquainted with at least the main spiritual trends of the latter, through St Ambrose, that fervent disciple of the Alexandrine mystics. He himself was a distinguished master of the spiritual life.

In the mind of the ancient writers, this mysticism was not yet isolated from other spiritual activities of the Christian life; rather was it the soul and sustenance of that life. It must be carefully discerned among the manifold activities in which they engaged, precisely in order to follow the promptings of Providence in the situations which demanded their intervention, and among the wealth of meditations inspired by their piety. Theology and philosophy often benefited from them, and this must not be forgotten when we approach these subjects. We must avoid becoming so preoccupied with these outward forms of thought that we overlook the deep religious inspiration often underlying them, or else despising them, under the pretext of delving deeper towards the divine core which is the source of their life.

The latter indeed is of prime importance for any true Christian who wishes to become acquainted with the Fathers and it is to this especially that we wish to draw attention in this work, which is a short collection of general studies on the thought of the Fathers. Nevertheless, insistence on their spirit can only be possible and profitable if we have a fairly clear general view of the body of literary work formed by patristic writings. We shall give here a summary of them which, short as it must be, is nevertheless indispensable if we are to classify adequately the very varied doctrinal material of which we are to attempt a synthesis. We shall have no difficulty in making out three fairly distinct groups: *The initiators*, in the first three centuries; the *great thinkers* of the fourth and fifth centuries, from St Athanasius to Leo the Great (†461); the *continuators*, from 461 to 843.

The first three centuries seem to be a preparatory period,

when we think of the prestige which the great Doctors of the fourth century were to enjoy. In point of fact, this period is of fundamental importance, for it fixes the foundations on which the imposing edifice of a pre-eminently spiritual character was subsequently to be built. In this respect, no doubt, one or other of the Fathers of the great century takes first rank; but in spite of certain gaps, the importance of which must not be exaggerated, the earliest Fathers have a very marked and lasting evangelical flavour about them. No doubt this is due to a more direct contact with apostolic times or to a more marked action of Providence in favour of the Church, still in its infancy and subject to persecution.

The great thinkers of ancient Christendom are to be found in the period which extends from the peace of Milan, 313, to the death of St Leo in 461, which was soon followed by the final fall of the Western Empire. These hundred and forty years, which for us constitute the great century of the Fathers, are not, as is often believed, a time of peace and easy triumph. Instead of an outward struggle, we now have a fight to save the faith carried on within the Church itself, and all the more serious for that. Divine Providence proffered aid in this struggle precisely by raising up in greater numbers men of superior quality who were to bring about the triumph of the orthodox Catholic tradition. Certain of these Doctors, such as St Basil of Caesarea, St Cyril of Alexandria in the east, St Ambrose in the west, did play a part in public affairs, but it would be quite wrong to regard them as political figures; they are above all Churchmen, as were St John Chrysostom and St Augustine, whose pre-eminently supernatural character is undisputed. All of them, in spite of varying modes of action imposed on them by circumstances, were men of the Church and instruments of the Holy Spirit.

Their continuators in the period extending from the fifth to the ninth century, were inevitably less illustrious: with St Leo, the great doctrinal inquiries are closed. The merit of the writers of the last patristic centuries was that, providentially, they were enabled to keep intact the sacred deposit, received from the

Apostles by the Church. In the west, more and more the papacy assumed the universal direction of the Church, and St Gregory the Great is the most perfect example of this high function of the Church and, through her, of the Holy Spirit in the world. In the east, the Byzantine Church, increasingly diminished by the Persian and Arab conquests, was closely linked to the Empire without, however, breaking its ties with Rome, thanks principally to the monks, those great defenders of the worship of Christ, devotion to the Blessed Virgin Mary, and the veneration of images, three focal points of their triumphant mysticism.

CHAPTER II

THE FATHERS, APPOINTED INSTRUMENTS OF THE SPIRIT IN THE MYSTICAL BODY

MEANING OF THE WORD "FATHERS"

We give the name of "Fathers of the Church" to all those Catholic writers of the first centuries whose work, in its broad outlines, conforms to traditional orthodoxy. The fact of having written does not in itself imply any special merit: their works are not included in the canonical Books of the Old and New Testaments, which are recognized as being divinely inspired. It is neither certain nor probable that the writings of the Fathers represent the entire sum of their personal activity, still less the total extent of apostolic activity in their time: far from it. Nevertheless, they have acquired exceptional authority in the eyes of succeeding centuries; for they provide us with direct evidence of the Christian life in its primitive forms. No doubt the communities grew and developed under an internal impulse, as a tree unfolds with the rising of the sap, and this is the sure sign of true vitality. But, without the help of the writings preserved from those times, we should have only a superficial knowledge of what this life was like. Hence the primordial interest in these works.

In point of fact, it is not until the fifth century that the word Father is widely used with the implication of doctrinal authority attributed to it today. St Basil and St Gregory Nazianzen were the initiators of this tendency. It became established at the time of the controversies over the nature of Christ, particularly at the Councils of Ephesus and Chalcedon (451). The fame of those bishops who had routed fourth-century heresies regarding the doctrine of the Trinity, by their action in or outside the Councils, but in any case by a true agreement in thought and in their religious attitude, then endowed the name of "Fathers" with a doctrinal importance which subsequently continued to grow. Its prestige is derived, not only from the great Councils of the fourth century, whose members were henceforth to be called Fathers, but also from previous bishops and even other Christians, as far back as apostolic times, who had received their approval.

Shortly after 430, St Vincent of Lérins, in his famous *Commonitorium*, appeals to the special authority of those who, being in communion with the whole Church, are the only "approved teachers" (*magistri probabiles*). They are those whom we call Fathers, very different from the simple ecclesiastical writers whose authority is not thus guaranteed. An important document of the end of the same century, partly the work of St Gelasius, to whom it was attributed in its entirety (the Gelasian Decree), clarifies this proposition and illustrates it by quoting famous names. One weighty name is missing, the most important of all for the origins, namely that of St Irenaeus, he who had set out the main rule in these matters : the necessity of conformity with the Apostolic See of Rome, alone capable of guaranteeing a direct link with the Apostles. This assertion of the authority of Rome tempered all that was too categorical or too personal in the work of St Vincent.

The holiness of life demanded in other respects as a qualification for the title of Father, is not of so rigorous a standard as that required by the canonization process with a view to liturgical honours; it demands truly worthy Christian life which need not necessarily have attained the heroic degree which the

Church gradually made an essential condition of elevation to the altars. In the title of Father, doctrinal orthodoxy takes precedence.

Antiquity is also a requisite in this field, and it goes back to the sources as far as, but excluding, the Apostles: the latter, indeed, are in some sort a continuation of the true Revelation which they directly witnessed in the person of Christ. This contact with the Apostles gives to the first Fathers, even if they are not bishops, and to the earliest writings, even if they remain anonymous, a very special authority, which must neither be exaggerated nor diminished. The beginning of the patristic period is therefore clearly fixed at the end of the first century, though Christian works of this period are rare: there is, however, one at least of prime importance, namely the Epistle of St Clement of Rome, and perhaps also the *Didache,* of which the author is unknown.

At the other extreme, the so-called patristic period was naturally less clearly defined. For a long time it has been considered as extending beyond the fifth century, and from the Middle Ages onwards special importance was attached to St Gregory the Great (†604) in the west, and in the east to St John Damascene, a simple monk and a priest in Jerusalem (†749), who was a sturdy defender of the veneration of images. In fact, these two dates are generally regarded as the limits. We do not think that the reasons put forward to fix these definite dates are decisive. It would mean excluding from the ranks of the Fathers saints who have an obvious affinity with Christian antiquity and who cannot without injustice be kept out, for their writings cannot be classified as being of medieval inspiration. For instance, in the east, St Theodore, who embodies the struggle against the iconoclasts at the beginning of the ninth century. Before him, in the west, stands out also the Venerable Bede, more than a century after St Gregory the Great, and we should, perhaps, associate with him the other great Anglo-Saxon monks of the early ninth century, who were much more witnesses of the past than real initiators.

In point of fact, the year 842, which saw the end of iconoclasm on the accession of the Empress Theodora, widow of the Emperor Theophilus and regent in the name of her son Michael who was still a minor, marks a capital date both in the religious and the political spheres, a date which is also emphasized by the Feast of Orthodoxy instituted in 843, and still observed in the Byzantine Church. Iconoclasm had only been defeated by the support of the west, in particular of the popes, and the new feast might have been called the feast of Catholic Orthodoxy: all the more reason to connect it with Christian antiquity. With the end of the ninth century a new historical era opens in the east as in the west. The patristic period is definitely closed.

SPIRITUAL WRITERS AND MYSTICS RATHER THAN SPECULATIVE THEOLOGIANS

The average modern reader approaches the Fathers with preoccupations very far removed from theirs and this prevents him from understanding them fully, in spite of an advanced literary and historical culture. He seeks from them information on points which they touched on only incidentally in connection with questions which to them were of much greater importance than those which interest the modern reader. There is a genuine patristic field of interest with which we must become acquainted in its broad outlines before approaching the works of the Fathers, if our study is to be a serious and objective one. Theologians themselves often go astray in this respect. All the more then does the layman run the risk of failing to penetrate into this special field, if he is not carefully informed on the subject.

The very title of this work, *Spiritual Writers and Mystics*, is not sufficient in itself to put the reader on the right track; these two words, useful and accurate as they are, have assumed in our time very precise meanings which correspond only vaguely with the ancient reality, though they do serve to set aside many false conceptions, hence the desirability of using them. Nevertheless, we must define them more closely, without, however, confining ourselves within too narrow a framework, which would prevent us from reaching the very core of these writings. The Fathers are less concerned with knowledge than with the living reality which is known by faith. But this reality alone sustains the soul of the Christian when it is enlightened by the Spirit, and the aim we have set ourselves in this basic study is to demonstrate the vital rôle which the Spirit plays.

In our analysis of this living reality we begin by pointing out that it is the Church, the continuation of Christ himself in this world, which is the dispenser of that life: the Church, whose direct action, prolonged through the centuries, the earliest Christian documents enable us to see and appreciate. It is a far cry indeed from St Clement of Rome and St Ignatius of Antioch to St Augustine and St Gregory the Great, but a powerful bond links them together, namely, the Mystical Body of Christ.

This Body, which is the Church, is, above all, the continued incarnation in this world of supernatural life properly so-called; it is a divine life in the fullest sense of the word. The conflict of the two cities, whose laws St Augustine set out in the fifth century, is already under way from the earliest time, and the apologists at the end of the second century are aware of what is at stake, or at least have glimpsed the grandeur and mystery of the struggle. They are not so much controversialists as apostles after their own fashion.

This note is still more marked in the case of the Doctors properly so-called, those who were granted the gift of penetrating to the heart of the divine mysteries, not indeed to grasp them fully, but to draw from them such enlightenment as was providentially required to combat the great heresies. They were pre-eminently contemplators of these mysteries, in the deepest sense of the word, and they found in this contemplation light and strength to carry out the great doctrinal mission entrusted to them by Providence in their own time.

The Doctors of the Church never failed to combine the strictest orthodoxy with the most intense Christian life, and the greatest of them were also ardent exponents of "living" faith. One may even say that this is the strongest common characteristic of the ancient writers: they were good shepherds, in the evangelical sense of the word.

All, without exception, gave themselves up to prayer with exemplary fervour and several of them were outstanding in this respect. Generally speaking, their mysticism has a doctrinal basis, but their faith was usually so closely bound up with charity that, in our time, it has sometimes been thought possible to emphasize only this second aspect of Christianity which leads to grave distortion. Religious experience is not excluded, but it reaches its peak in pure contemplation of the true God, and even of the Trinity. The Three Persons, without in any way losing their transcendent character, enter into real communication with souls in prayer, and the ancient Doctors seem frequently to have enjoyed this privilege, so much do their works bear witness to a certain intimacy with them.

This mysticism is inseparable from a real asceticism, which serves as its basis, and it must not be forgotten here, though the doctrinal principles of a complete or autonomous ascetic method were formulated and systematized only much later. Very often, such a synthesis becomes possible only after a long experimental period and sometimes in reaction against abuses, just as, on the doctrinal level, dogmatic definitions and the building up of systems have only been achieved in answer to errors.

Some attempts at theological systematization were made by the Fathers, but they are exceptional. The early writers were concerned less with knowledge and its rigorous demands in respect of method, than with life in the various forms to which we have just referred. There were a few attempts, in the east, before St Augustine, who, at the beginning of the fifth century or just before, produced several outline treatises, masterly in themselves, and four centuries later, patristic writings were enriched by the small doctrinal synthesis of St John Damascene. All this points forward to a vast field of exploration. It was worked over in the Middle Ages by means of a new method, no longer that of the Fathers, but it must not make us forget theirs.

Students of the works of the Fathers have tended to neglect

their philosophy and this leaves a definite gap, especially in the case of the greatest of them. No doubt it is true that for them and for the eastern Fathers especially, philosophy remains a secondary field. Nevertheless it is useful to remember it, if only to bear in mind that it plays a subordinate rôle which is often overestimated. Others, it is true, minimize its importance too much, especially as regards the west. Here, however, St Augustine, from the time of his conversion, took a place in philosophy which, though it is always of secondary importance for him, cannot be neglected without grave detriment to his memory, and still more so to the history of western and Christian thought. St Augustine was a thinker in the highest sense of the word, but a religious thinker, the supreme example of the saint who, after his conversion, abandoned himself body and soul to grace, and who, for centuries, has remained the supreme spiritual guide of the west.

This methodical analysis, which will find its detailed justification in the following chapters, confirms our definition of the Fathers given at the beginning of this work: appointed instruments of the Holy Spirit in that privileged period of Christian Antiquity, an age upon which Christ showered his gifts so that it should become the supreme guide of the new era.

THE MAIN FEATURE OF THE PATRISTIC WRITINGS: CHRISTIAN WISDOM

The foregoing condensed outline is in danger of giving a very jejune impression of the history of teaching which was, before all else, a Christian way of life of the highest kind, for institutions as well as for individuals. If we are to characterize it with a single word we might perhaps sum it all up in the term Christian wisdom, regarding this as an inner realization of living faith acting through charity, as St Paul says (Gal. 5. 6): here, taking all in all, we are faced with a perfect achievement. The Church had to achieve this perfection in order to make her mark, as she did, in these first Christian centuries: for everything had to be newly created, in the spiritual sphere, in a world rendered materialistic by paganism and by a powerful but implacable government. It was necessary to reach out beyond the body, and make the spirit live by turning it towards a God who is pure in spirit, absolutely transcendent, and yet capable of implanting in man a higher life, first in his own soul and then, as it were, by reason of its superabundance, in the souls of others.

Such is the great law of the Gospel. Christ filled the Apostles with his Spirit to enable them to undertake the conquest of the world. He had acted and preached before them for years; he had appeared to them after his resurrection, and still they remained hesitant, stupefied, as it were, so much, no doubt, did they feel overwhelmed by a superhuman task. The Holy Spirit at Pentecost made different men of them, first transforming them inwardly, and it was the strength of this inward renewal which subsequently acted on the whole of humanity like the leaven in dough, according to the saying of our Saviour himself. This action of the Spirit of God on man takes many forms. But all of them tend towards a universal wisdom, which is, as it were, a synthesis of the theological virtues and the higher gifts of the Holy Spirit. That is the core of the Gospel spirit with which the Fathers were imbued and which was to be the true sustenance of their activity.

We must take care not to think of them primarily as philosophers, as those who judge them only from one point of view, in order to condemn them, appear to imagine. In many of them, a real effort of reasoning can be seen, but it is subordinate and not essential, as some people of our time seem to think. Reason plays only an auxiliary rôle in their theology. And, for them, theology itself is less a science, in the technical sense of the word, than a conscious life of faith organized for their personal benefit and that of their fellow beings; for the Fathers, most of whom held high responsibility for souls entrusted to their care, were bound to instruct and mould them. Thus, several of them, at least, laid the foundation of a true Christian theology and even of a certain philosophy.

However, that is not the essence of the patristic soul. The

Fathers were, first and foremost, witnesses of a transcendent God, who nevertheless loves his creatures to the extent of making his dwelling in humanity, and even in each individual human being, through Christ and his Spirit. In other words, God, out of love for us, deigns to dwell in the Church, that portion of humanity gathered together by Christ in the person of the Apostles which he enlivens with his Spirit. That is the special province of the Fathers, the fundamental feature of their teaching and their activity.

The Fathers are the men of the Spirit and the witnesses of his active presence in the womb of humanity. They are not wild visionaries, frail playthings of their imagination or of their wandering senses. They are men of sound mind, as is demonstrated by the continuity, power and fertility of their work. In point of fact, they spread to the furthest corners of the earth that unrivalled force which is Christianity. It brought about a spiritual transformation in humanity; it is the only force which counts today in the face of materialism organized for the exploitation of the world in denial of the true ends of man. The Spirit, in the highest sense of the word, at once sets us on a higher plane, binding together in perfect harmony the varied aspects of man's lofty capacity in the Christian order.

In order to avoid dangerous misconceptions we must define broadly the various meanings of the word *spirit*. It is often used to denote the human soul, regarded from the point of view of its suprasensual activity, its sublime intuitive insights and its rational life. Without in any way detracting from the essential unity of man as body and soul, the necessary subordination of the body to the soul can be emphasized. The action of the senses in the soul is very different from the higher activities which we call supernatural, but there is no duality involved. Certain of the Fathers made too wide a distinction between them; but others, like St Augustine, are careful to safeguard the unity of the soul, at the same time directing its spiritual faculties towards a supreme spiritual Being who is God and who, moreover, remains transcendent. God in his fullness is Spirit, pure Spirit, although he is everywhere and in every creature by virtue of his very being and of his activity. It is the Holy Spirit who is the principle of the divine activity in souls. This action takes place mainly in the supernatural order. The term Christian spirit aptly denotes a true spiritual collaboration between man and God in accordance with the principles laid down by Christ and put into effect with the help of the Holy Spirit. We shall confine ourselves to these fundamental meanings of the term.

In the sphere of action the whole can perhaps be summed up in the word wisdom, taking this word in the higher sense which immediately carries us to a plane where the divine and the human meet, in the realm of thought as well as in that of the apostolate. It is a living wisdom, divine wisdom, a true synthesis of the three great virtues which are the basis of Christianity, according to St Paul (1 Cor. 13. 1–13). The scientific wisdom of later theologians was to lay greater emphasis on speculative principles, which are indeed necessary for all inquirers, even in the supernatural field, with whatever adaptations may be required in the study of the supernatural. It excludes none of the principles laid down by the Fathers on another plane: the living practice of faith, hope and charity under the impulse of the Holy Spirit.

CHAPTER III

THE FATHERS, CHURCHMEN

IN THE HIGHEST SENSE

THE CHURCH AS THE TEMPLE OF THE LIVING GOD

Clearly, the title of Churchmen is the first which we must emphasize when speaking of those generally called Fathers of the Church. It must be understood primarily in the spiritual sense, not that this excludes the doctrinal aspect, far from it, but it has a fuller meaning, at least in the case of those first witnesses with whom we are dealing.

St Ignatius of Antioch, who died about the year 107, after a long episcopate in the city where St Peter had resided for a number of years, is known to us only through seven letters written to various Churches, in the course of his journey to Rome, where he suffered that martyrdom for which he longed. They are not classical masterpieces, but the religious fervour which inspired them is so noble and so powerful that many pages attain great heights of eloquence, whether he is singing the praises of Christ and the Church, harrying the heretics or exhorting the faithful to the purest spiritual life. The central idea of this teaching is clearly the Church, regarded primarily as the temple of the living God. In his writings, we find the Christian community already well organized, with the essentials of its hierarchy (bishops, priests and deacons), including the authority of the central See, situated in "the noble and holy Church, which holds the primacy", and is clearly designated as Rome: for the saint already possesses an informed sense of universality, and himself finds the word "catholic" to express it. But however fruitful such a message may be from the institutional point of view, to employ a technical term, nothing in the writings of the saints can compare with this great Syrian martyr's fervour and power of eloquence.

The generation of which St Ignatius is the most illustrious representative, is less preoccupied with the Parousia than that which produced the *Didache*; it prefers to concentrate on the spiritual and mystical presence of the Saviour. Thus we find a fine series of suggestive formulas: "Let us perform all our actions with the thought that God lives in us; thus we will be his temples and he will be our God, dwelling within us" (Eph. 15. 3). Thus he calls the Christians *theophores, naophores, christophores, hagiophores*, and that, no doubt, is the reason why at the beginning of each letter, he loves to recall his second name of Theophorus. God makes known his presence in us to those who love him (Eph. 15); it is the fruit of faith and charity: faith and charity, he says, are the beginning and the end of life; faith is its beginning, charity its perfection, the union of the two is God himself (Eph. 14).

This inner life rests on a sublime knowledge of Christ, not only as man, but as God, a knowledge so intense and so penetrating that it has something of the character of a vision. It is this knowledge, the perfection of faith, which the mystics were later to call contemplation. St Ignatius did not expound the theory of it as Clement of Alexandria or St Augustine did at a later date, but he lived by it, and that is the most important thing, for this spiritual knowledge was intended to assist the flowering of the perfect Christian life. The latter blossoms into apostolic zeal, and no one urged Christians, priests or laymen, to it with more fervour than the saint. In his letters to the eastern Churches he issues directives of astonishing power and fruitfulness.

Nor is there any trace of conceit in this man; in speaking of himself he uses words of self-abasement which leave no doubt as to the state of his soul: in all truth, he considers himself insignificant and unworthy to be counted among the members of Christ. These expressions occur frequently; but the finest example is to be found in the Epistle to the Romans, whom St Ignatius urgently begs not to bar the way to martyrdom for him: "to die" in order to "go to Christ", that is his one desire, and he proclaims it in letters of fire.

Compared with this ardour, the Epistle of St Clement of Rome († *circa* 100) to the Corinthians seems a little "colourless". But it would be a mistake to overemphasize the contrast. This document was written by the Bishop of Rome in quite different circumstances, with a very special end in view. His task was to lay the foundations of an interior reorganization in a Church troubled by factions, hence a broad summary of principles in a long, almost didactic treatise which is nevertheless by no means lacking in warmth; then a clear recall to the order established by God in the Christian community, followed by an injunction to renounce those divisions which had torn apart the members of Christ.

This doctrinal aspect of the question is treated at length throughout the Epistle. The practice of virtue is based on the example of the Saviour who has redeemed us by suffering (c. 16), on the mission of Christ as priest and redeemer (c. 36), on the institution by him of a hierarchy (c. 42), and precisely that hierarchy which has been desecrated in Corinth and which must be restored (c. 51–3); but still more as a priest appealing to the highest religious sentiments, in an exhortation recalling the primitive liturgy and showing the saint's acute awareness of the living presence of Christ in the Church.

There is no trace here, nor in St Ignatius, of belief in an approaching Parousia (imminent return of Christ), such as can be found in the *Didache* (c. 16) or in the so-called Epistle of St Barnabas (c. 21), writings which must be assigned to a slightly earlier period (the end of the first century). Moreover, there may be discerned in them an impression, a hope, desire or aspiration, rather than any definite teaching. The latter is clearly formulated towards the end of the second century, but then it has a source other than the words of Christ: it arose out of Montanism which was based on a revelation, of the Spirit, speaking through a new prophet, Montanus. Even a new convert like Tertullian was drawn to it after some years of pure and fruitful activity within the traditional framework. Even in his error, he testifies to the important place held in the primitive conception of the Church by the doctrine of the presence of God living in her through Christ and the Spirit.

St Cyprian (†258), a compatriot of Tertullian and his disciple, did not follow him in his error. On the contrary, as Bishop of Carthage, he insisted on the rôle of the hierarchy against the *lapsi,* those Christians who had fallen away in the Decian persecution (250) and who claimed the right to be absolved by the "spirituals" alone. Yet he himself, as regards the unity of the whole Church, does not seem to have fully understood the requirements of the traditional doctrine. He recognizes the unique importance of the See of Rome and even gave it expression in the finest traditional formulas. However, no doubt unconsciously, he relied too exclusively on the Holy Spirit to maintain this unity, whereas tradition, already very clear in his time, added to the action of the Spirit that of a See specially appointed to safeguard it.

THE APOSTOLIC SEE, THE CENTRE OF THE CHURCH

From the beginning of the second century, the See of Rome plays an important part in the Church, witness St Ignatius and St Clement. At the end of the same century, the action of Victor I (189–99) brings it into broad relief. But the principle itself is expressly formulated in a passage of incomparable clarity. It is that of St Irenaeus, Bishop of Lyons at the end of the 2nd century († *circa* 201), and occurs at the beginning of Book III, in a treatise *Against Heresies* which comprises five books. It is therefore fundamental and, in fact, lays down a rule of universal application. Here is the substance of it: "We set forth the faith of the very great and very ancient Church founded in Rome by the two most glorious Apostles Peter and Paul, in order to confound those who take their stand against the right. With this Church indeed, because of her pre-eminent authority, every other Church must agree, in which the tradition coming from the Apostles has been preserved." This rule is one of dazzling clarity to the unbiased mind. It must not be understood in such a way as to exclude all appeal to Scripture: the link with the Apostles affirms the exact opposite. But its aim is to simplify and generalize the appeal to Scripture by a secure and universal rule: namely, doctrinal union with the Apostolic See. This theological aspect is not the only one, and discipline is not excluded; but the dominant thought in the Bishop of Lyons's work is clearly dogmatic.

In Latin Africa, fifty years later, St Cyprian himself echoed St Irenaeus in terms almost as clear regarding the principle involved. In his treatise on "The Unity of the Church" (250) the Bishop of Carthage lays down principles which recall those of St Irenaeus, but here applied to discipline as well as dogma: he reminds us that the universal Church is founded on Peter, by the ordinance of Christ himself, who "established the Church on a single" Apostle (*super unum aedificavit Ecclesiam*), and, by virtue of this formula, he has been called "the first theorist of catholicity". More important still, perhaps, is this other formula from the same work: "We cannot have God for our Father if we have not the Church for our Mother." In a more or less contemporary epistle (Ep. 59) he speaks of "the Chair of Peter" as "the principal Church", at least in the sense that "in it the unity of the priesthood has its origin", and this is a far-reaching statement. It is true that the saint does not seem to have understood all the requirements implied by this principle, hence certain painful conflicts with the Bishops of Rome themselves. Nevertheless, he recognized the principle and he was far from being its initiator. He was merely echoing St Irenaeus and tradition. The life of the Church is in itself the truest indication of the importance of this principle.

At about the same time, in the east, St Dionysius, Bishop of Alexandria, a staunch enemy of the heretics of his country, employed in his struggle against the modalism of Sabellius (Modalism considered the divine persons as simple modalities, thus virtually denying the Trinity in God), formulas which, from another point of view, were as dangerous as his, for, contrary to the intentions of the author, they led to a real subordination of the Son and the denial of his divinity. The Bishop of Rome, St Dionysius, was informed, and he called the great Alexandrine bishop to order. The latter gave him full satisfaction, without in any way appealing to the apostolicity of his own Church, after Rome, one of the greatest in Christendom. Thus we see that the apostolicity of the See of Peter possessed effective authority proportionate with its dignity.

In the following century, another great Bishop of Alexandria, St Athanasius, found himself in difficulties with the Arians in the reign of Constantine, and again under his successor; exiled, he had recourse to Rome, where the Pope exercised his authority to good effect and had him restored to his episcopal city. All his life he remained attached to the Apostolic See in which he saw, as it were, an extension of the incarnate Word, for that was the aspect of Christianity which impressed him most. This great adversary of the Arians, who was bemused with philosophy, did not follow these heretics on to their own ground : he had only one weapon against them, the Incarnation of the Word, which he saw in the person of Christ and in every Christian. Hence his preoccupation with the Church, the work of Christ and his very Body. This last feature is a central one in the teaching of St Athanasius. He had stated the essentials of it in his earliest writings, and the conflict with the Arians led him to develop it considerably. It has been said that he saw a close, even physical connection between the Incarnation of the Word and the deification of man. In Jesus the Word penetrates his humanity and also, in some sense, ours. Thus humanity is closely linked with him. In him the Word has "wordified" us so that our deification is connected with his Incarnation. Such is the general trend of a doctrine which connects dogma closely with life, just as it associates eternal wisdom and created wisdom. Soaring to these heights, the living theology of St Athanasius escaped from the quibbles of the baptized philosophers and won the day for the Catholic doctrine of the Incarnate Word. His providential action was decisive.

THE CATHOLICITY OF THE ANCIENT CHURCH

The message of Christ, sending his Apostles to preach to the whole world, *in universum mundum* (Mark 16. 15), was summed up by the Fathers in the word "Catholic". St Ignatius uses it as early as the beginning of the second century to denote either the universal Church, or any individual Church which by the faith common to all is related body and soul to the whole world: *Smyrna*, 1 and 8; *Ephesus*, n. 3. The use of the word Catholic becomes general in the fourth century; it occurs in the Creeds of Nicaea, Jerusalem and Constantinople in the east and in that of Rome. St Cyril of Jerusalem uses it in his Catecheses (18. 26). In the west, St Irenaeus in the text quoted above (p. 33) identified catholicity with union with Rome, without actually employing the word himself.

St Augustine, on the other hand, makes forceful use of it, as St Optatus had already done: he exclaims triumphantly against the Donatists: "We Catholics are to be found throughout the whole world, for we are in communion with all the earth, in every place where the glory of Christ has penetrated" (*In Ps*. 56, n. 13). St Epiphanius used the double formula, "Catholic and Apostolic Church", in the creed which terminates his great work on faith (*Anchoratus*), and indeed the terms are all but synonymous, according to the rule of faith well known in antiquity.

The particular shade of meaning implied in the word *Catholic* is perhaps to be sought less in the sense of actual extent than in that of fitness to embrace the whole world. Thus the word supplements the idea of apostolicity, which looks back to the origins of the Christian movement. Catholicity excludes any excessive local attachments which are opposed to the true universality of the Gospel message. The Donatist schismatics gloried in being Africans, and St Augustine points out to them the absurdity of their pretensions. Elsewhere, he observes with noble firmness what strength the Catholic draws from this awareness of having the whole world on one's side: "That is why the whole world confidently withholds its approval from those who hold themselves apart from the whole world, in whatever region of the earth" (*Against the Epistle of Parmenianus*, III, p. 24). The grave tone of this simple sentence made a salutary impression on Newman and brought about his final decision to make the sacrifices demanded by his return to the full faith. He, like so many others, had been held back by excessive local attachments which weigh on the soul and prevent it from embracing the universal horizons opened up by pure Catholicism. It was on these horizons that the eyes of souls were fixed in the time of the Fathers and on which, with a few rare exceptions, the Fathers themselves gazed, already obliged as they were to combat schisms and heresies. The outstanding example is St Augustine, whose zeal finally won the day against that Donatism which, for a whole century, was the scourge of Latin Africa.

In the case of St Ambrose, the Catholic note takes on a very special tone. Beginning as adviser to the western Emperors, then to Theodosius the Great who had become sole ruler of the Empire, united then for the last time, he obtained for the Church total recognition of her independence in the religious sphere, without prejudice to the imperial power which remains sole judge in its own sphere: the Emperor accepted the bishop's remonstrances in a true Christian spirit and did penance publicly, which, far from diminishing imperial authority, even enhanced it in the public esteem, so skilful was the bishop in combining authority with tact in the purely moral and religious sphere. The great bishop who himself had once been a high-ranking servant of the State, as he now was of the Church, obtained for that Church privileges constituting a homage of the temporal to the spiritual, without either usurpation or abuse of power; for with paganism in decline, the ancient privileges of the State religion automatically fell to her; and now, indeed, the true religion was that of the most important servants of the State, even in the highest ranks of the imperial hierarchy.

This aspect of St Ambrose's Catholicism must not cause us to forget his profoundly religious soul and his entire devotion to the moral and spiritual apostolate; that he was a mystic is shown by his writings on virginity which for centuries stimulated and sustained the fervour of Christian women dedicated to God.

The note of Marian piety is traditionally associated with St Cyril of Alexandria, because of his defence of the divine maternity against Nestorius of Constantinople, who denied it. The term *Theotokos*, Mother of God, was popular in Byzantium and when this new bishop, who came from Antioch, let it be publicly decried and decried it himself, there was a real conflict between the two great prelates and, for the second time, a bishop of Constantinople coming from Antioch was deposed by a bishop of Alexandria, or at least with his active intervention. Obviously, it would be rash to regard this as no more than a local struggle, prompted by vanity and intrigue. The conflict was one of importance to Christendom and its dramatic climax and dénouement can be clearly seen at Ephesus, in 431.

St Cyril, a real theologian and one of the most profound thinkers in the Alexandrine tradition, immediately recognized the full importance of the conflict. To refuse Mary the title of Mother of God (*Theotokos*) amounts to denying the Incarnation, for, if the Word is truly incarnate, he is God-Man (or Man-God in one single Person; but not God and man as if there were two persons). Mary is truly the Mother of the Man-God, and not of the man only. The whole theology of the Incarnation was thus at stake, and St Cyril pointed out the links in the chain one by one. His theses were approved by Pope St Celestine I and he received authorization to obtain the adhesion of Eastern Africa to his formulas. A council having met at Ephesus on his instigation and that of the Pope, he attended it with a strong group of suffragans, thus making sure of a good majority. By his efforts, the approval of the papal legates was obtained and Nestorius was condemned. Mary was proclaimed "Mother of God" and St Cyril, triumphant, spoke of a "physical" union of God and man in Christ.

The "Monophysism" of Eutyches was the clumsy and crude expression of an oversimplified realism, tending to neglect the human nature of Christ in favour of the divine nature, which was identified with the person. The true theologians of this group were able to avoid confusion only by the use of subtle distinctions. Once again the Pope intervened: St Leo himself contributed directly to the choice of the definitive formula: "One and the same Christ . . . in two natures", by which the Church finally expressed, in the minimum of words, the substance of the mystery of the Incarnation. The expression was apt in its brevity. It was eventually adopted, though not without difficulty. Whole sections of Christendom resisted, less from love of orthodoxy than for political motives. They put themselves outside the pale of Catholicity by their adherence to local formulas or personal viewpoints, to the detriment of the traditional faith which St Leo represented with unrivalled prestige and authority. In this case, and throughout his pontificate, he was the true embodiment of the whole Catholic Church. By his doctrinal as well as his pastoral work, he fully merited the name of Great.

Shortly after his death the Western Empire fell, but the papacy, which he had rendered so illustrious, continued for a long time to benefit from his prestige, and this strength was a blessing for the new peoples, who themselves were gradually absorbed into Catholicism. The popes retained a high degree of spiritual authority in the midst of the universal disorder caused by the arrival of the barbarians. Another pope, St Gregory, also called the Great, was to strive successfully to bring these peoples one by one into the bosom of the Catholic Church, and the latter found in her fidelity to the traditional faith a strength capable of transforming the customs of the uncivilized invaders. The greatness of the bishops of this time and especially of those writers whom we call Fathers, however modest their literary ability, is to be found in their adherence to that profound religious tradition which we call Catholic: it possessed the strength to create a certain order out of the chaos of the west.

The Eastern Empire at its centre, by dint of courage and political sense, resisted providentially the encroachment of the

Persians and later of the Arabs, though not without losing important provinces. With the aim of defending their realm, a true stronghold of Christianity, the emperors drew the bishops into predominantly worldly activities, to the detriment of universality, especially in the seventh and eighth centuries; but the Catholic sense was never stifled in the best of them and the Byzantine Fathers of this period were still strong defenders of the Catholic faith, particularly in the field of Marian theology, of which they remain the best witnesses, and in the promotion of the veneration of images with St Germanus, St John Damascene and St Theodore the Studite.

THE CHURCH AND THE CITY OF GOD

The various aspects of the Church, which we have just described by referring to their greatest exponents, are all three pre-eminently spiritual. But there is one, still vaster and more sublime, which forms a synthesis of the three and embellishes them in a special way: this is the theme of the "City of God", to which St Augustine devoted the greatest and most famous of his works, after the *Confessions* and treatise on the Trinity. In the latter, the saint shows us God, God in Three Persons, taking possession of his soul, in spite of his own resistance: for if sin abounded in him so much more did grace abound. What he had observed in himself and powerfully described in the long meditations, prayers and searchings at the beginning of his episcopate, St Augustine returned to in a broader sense fifteen years later, after 410, when he meditated on the fate of the Empire and of the whole of humanity, after the sack of Rome by the Visigoths; for the *City of God* is above all a prolonged meditation on the place of man in the universe and his deep longing for that eternal life which alone merits the name of "City of God".

This city is characterized primarily by a spirit, which draws its true strength from the love of God, if this love predominates to the extent of embracing all the aspirations of man and guiding him in all his actions. He succeeds precisely to the extent in which he restrains his egoism or baser self-seeking.

To bring out the salient features of this "celestial" city, he shows it in conflict with a force, less constructive no doubt, but capable too of directing human activities within a group which has some affinity with the preceding one; it too may, in certain respects, be called a city: it is the "terrestrial" city regarded from the point of view of its basic principles, particularly self-love. Hence this assertion, which is the main theme of the work: "Two loves, therefore, have built two cities: the one *terrestrial*, fruit of the love of self to the contempt of God; the other *celestial*, fruit of the love of God to the contempt of self" (*City of God*, bk. 14, ch. 28).

In the opening lines of this work, Augustine calls the City of God "most glorious" (*gloriosissima*). For him the essence of this city lies in the future life: "as it exists in the permanence of that eternal abiding place, which it now awaits in patience (Rom. 8. 25) till justice be turned into judgement (Ps. 93. 15) and which it will fully obtain one day in final victory and perfected peace". However, he must still contemplate it at length, "in the present course of time where it walks, sustained by faith among the impious" (*City of God*, bk. 1, ch. 1). And in the early books, especially in those five which form, as it were, a broad portico to the vast edifice under construction, he goes on to enumerate the tendencies of earthly cities, whose spirit differs so much from that of the other, for in them pride and lust for power hold sway (*ibid.*).

The first book is a general answer intended to restore the faithful, who, on the one hand, were disturbed by the horrors perpetrated by the Visigoths in the city they had conquered and, on the other hand, by the plaintive regrets of the pagans mourning for their gods. Augustine points out that this is no final catastrophe in the eyes of faith, as long as there is no real moral collapse, and that the grievances of the idolators have even less foundation than those of the Christians, for paganism had made no attempt to forestall such a catastrophe. This theme is developed in the three books which follow, wherein the vices of the ancient Romans are described with an eloquent wealth of detail, only too justified in fact. In the fifth book

Augustine passes from this *argumentum ad hominem* to general questions touching the cause of Roman greatness which, though undisputed, must nevertheless be judged in the light of God. He goes so far as to encourage Christians by reminding them of the virtues on which the strength of the Empire was founded (ch. 15–16): if God thus rewarded human virtues radically vitiated by self-love, how much more would he take account of the supernatural virtues, provided they were pure. The Roman Empire was the work of Providence (ch. 21). And the book closes with a eulogy of the two great Christian emperors of the fourth century, Constantine and Theodosius (ch. 25–6). In this complex apologetic, St Augustine keeps both orders steadily in view and still more so the two eras, so to speak: that of time which passes away and in which we live; that of eternity which lies in store and towards which we are travelling.

This masterly treatise continues (in Bks. 6–10) in another synthesis based on a higher apologetic of a mainly doctrinal order. Augustine here makes an acute criticism of the speculations of the ancients and of Greco-Roman religion, but he does not neglect to point out many of its loftier elements which Christian revelation was able to put to good use. The Platonic school of philosophy receives all the author's sympathy, and he dwells on it (in Bk. 8). He even attributes to Plato, his favourite philosopher, many personal observations which his own genius, enlightened by faith, added to the views of the Athenian thinker, as transmitted by Plotinus.

The twelve succeeding books which set out, in three parts, the origin (11–14), the development (15–18) and the end of the City of God (19–22) are mainly devoted to a description of the supernatural order which God has willed to create within humanity. The natural and philosophical aspects of the subject are not neglected, particularly in his study of the origins; but the divine note is all-pervading and remains predominant until there emerges the celebrated idea of the two cities which concludes the first section (Bk. 15, ch. 28). History predominates in the second phase and, in the third, doctrine again comes to the fore. To whatever heights the saint's thought soars, we admire particularly (in Bk. 19) his penetrating observations on the interaction of the two cities with a view to a peace which he envisages not only on a universal metaphysical plane (*tranquillitas ordinis*), but also on a human and social plane (*ordinata concordia*). The latter formula implies a whole programme of Christian action in this world. But this point of view, though important, remains secondary by comparison with the supreme realities towards which humanity is invincibly directed by faith, and which are dealt with in the last three books: the end of the world, the last judgement, the punishment of the damned in hell and the joy of the elect in that heaven which is the true city of God (Bks. 20–2), only these vast and lofty horizons could fully satisfy the great Doctor's religious and human aspirations.

It is the Church which is directly and exclusively responsible for the supernatural order we have just described. Her very constitution, established by Christ, makes her perfectly fitted for this. She is no angelic society, but a human society, corporeal in certain respects but spiritual in others, and this aspect is always predominant. She is apostolic, founded on a tradition which goes back to the origins of Christianity; she is catholic, that is to say, universal as regards her sphere of activity which transcends national interests; finally she stands above even the State, in the supernatural sphere which is her appointed end, without in any way purposing to rule the State, but nevertheless demanding of it that recognition to which her mission entitles her. It is true that in the Middle Ages she may have accepted or demanded some authority of a human kind, the social conditions of the time permitting or even requiring this, in order to ensure her necessary independence. These demands were supported by an appeal to *The City of God*, wrongly no doubt, for the Augustinian viewpoint is confined to a much higher level, but the motives involved and the social conditions at that time might have justified this appeal to doctrines of another order: "Augustinian politics" are Augustinian only in a very broad sense, more spiritual than political.

CHAPTER IV

THE CONTEMPLATORS OF THE "GREAT MYSTERIES"

PIONEERS OF THE SPIRITUAL LIFE

All revealed truths are "mysteries", in the sense that their existence cannot be established by reason alone; they are known only by revelation. This is the primary meaning of the word and of those realities which we call mysteries: God alone can fully understand them, or even reveal them, by whatever means he sees fit to employ, and these are of infinite variety. Though these truths cannot be fully understood by us, we can grasp them in part, and that is why we are invited to take them as themes of meditation and study to enrich our life of prayer. All revealed truths can, in some way, provide food for the Christian life. Certain of them, however, have a special value in this respect, that is why we call them the great mysteries; their greatness is relative to our shortcomings but real in relation to the aspirations of the heart towards the infinite, aspirations which the great mysteries gratify to the full with a divine abundance.

By a dispensation of Providence, the Doctors of the great patristic century were drawn, more than those of other periods, towards these sublime divine realities, not out of vain curiosity, but because they grasped them in a high degree with an understanding which, though relative, was nonetheless profound. To realize the importance of these mysteries in our life requires a great gift of God. Of the men of this time who were granted that gift, the greatest were bishops, and without seeking to do so they added to the title of pastor that of master in the divine sciences, for they lived them first of all in prayer. It can be said of the great Doctors that they were true "contemplators" of the highest mysteries before proclaiming them to the world.

St Irenaeus (†201) was a real pioneer in this field. It is true that, before him, St Ignatius of Antioch had shown a profound knowledge of Christ. But it was not given to him to set out the treasures of this mystery in the same way as the Doctors. He was a mystic and a man of action rather than a master thinker. In this respect, the Bishop of Lyons, who, like him, came from the east, opened up wider horizons to the thought of primitive Christianity. A native of Asia who had come to Gaul as a missionary, he succeeded St Pothinus, who himself had come from the east, in 178. He devoted the greater part of his life, until his death in about 201, to combating the Gnostics. The Gnostic heresy, too, came from the east; it followed the Christian movement everywhere and strove to infect it with its dualist theories, under the cloak of religion. Irenaeus wrote mainly in Greek, his mother tongue, and his principal work, *Against Heresies*, is one of the monuments of Christian litera- ture in that language. The work comprises five books. Its style is simple but it is full of information of the highest value, and it remains our principal source of information on the Gnostic heresy in the west, its origins and its forms. In the last three books he turns against it a series of closely-reasoned arguments, and the work is, at the same time, a doctrinal exposition with- out equal for its period. St Irenaeus would have been inscribed in the highest ranks of the official list of Doctors of the Church if the liturgically superior title of Martyr had not hitherto prevented it. This doctrinal character of his writings has been brought into prominence in the last fifty years by the discovery of his *Proof of the Apostolic Preaching*, in which the saint sets out the traditional faith without any controversial aim, but simply to edify and instruct. The common people found in it the substance of the earlier treatise and theologians quote it, but without forgetting the main treatise which, from a doctrinal point of view, remains the outstanding work of this period.

The third century was to witness the appearance of many

others, some of them of considerable value, but almost all of them, by some noteworthy omission, testify to the fact that the religious culture of the time was still in a state of formation. Christian thinkers were feeling their way, and we must wait until the fourth century before we find works which are definitive in any given field.

These omissions are very obvious in the case of Tertullian, one of the greatest figures of the third century. From the time of his conversion he plunged into apologetics and to a greater degree into the doctrinal controversy, and moral and spiritual activities. His work is full of intuitions of genius and illuminating flashes, but too often balance is lacking in this man who is so well aware of his own greatness. Here we can confine ourselves to consideration of his essential dogmatic positions. Their basis is a sound one: namely, the revelation contained in Scripture. He is firm in reserving all control of it to the hierarchy and his argument takes on a judicial rigour in the *Liber de prescriptione haereticorum*: only the Church can say of Scripture: "It belongs to me; I have long possessed it; I have priority; I have solid foundations going back to the original owners. I am the heir to the Apostles" (ch. 37). The heretics possess no guarantee but the devil and his minions. These principles are invoked particularly against Gnostics of all shades, and especially the partisans of Marcion, Hermogenes and Valentinus. Tertullian supplements Irenaeus in defending the unity of God, questioned by this paganism renewed as a result of eastern speculation, and strong enough to invade the west.

Tertullian even touches on the theory of the Trinity, which remained in the background of the controversies until victory over idolatry was assured, thought it could not escape the curiosity of certain minds. The boldest of them explained the diversity of the three persons in God, particularly the Father and the Son, as being merely two aspects (modalities), the Son being only a special way of looking at God who is one in person and in nature: the persons, they said with Sabellius, are different aspects of the same nature, not true realities in themselves. This "modalism" was often given the name of Sabellianism after Sabellius who was its principal exponent.

Tertullian was particularly severe in his attacks on Praxeas, one of the great representatives of the sect in the west, and he waged war on it with remarkably ingenious and subtle arguments. Latin thought was later to benefit from them and, thanks to him, was able to offer greater resistance to the subtleties of Arianism in the following century. The African master was all the more eager in this dispute since it concerned a doctrine particularly dear to him, but in which he himself later went astray, through excessive attachment to the person of the Holy Spirit.

THE GREAT DOCTORS OF THE EAST

In spite of their greatness, the masters prior to the fourth century are only precursors compared with those which we find in this new and, in a sense, decisive period. The fundamental dogmas of Christianity were questioned by great minds, more addicted to reasoning than belief. This severe trial, however, had the effect of making clearer than in the past the capital importance of certain truths on which, on a last analysis, not only the Christian creed, but all Christian life depend.

From this point of view, the example of St Athanasius is particularly illuminating. He was by no means a specialist dwelling in solitary meditation on a particular point of doctrine, yet it is true that there was a moment when, almost unaided, he held in check the whole force of Arianism, massed against the council of Nicaea, because he had understood the capital importance of the rôle played in the Christian Faith by a *Man-God* in the fullest sense of the word, and because he defended this doctrine with indomitable power against its opponents. It is clear that in doing this he was aided by God. He asserts first of all, or rather he worships, three Persons in God, and he proclaims his faith with a vigour till then unequalled : three Persons, quite distinct, but nevertheless fundamentally one, in one indivisible substance. Basing his arguments on Scripture, without any speculative investigation, which he considered superfluous in such a field, and opposed by thinkers of great pride and subtlety who could not be prevailed upon to compromise, he ceaselessly reiterated the basic truths of the faith in the very words of Scripture, aided by comparisons which would be familiar to the people of Alexandria. It is not the *homo-ousios* which is the focal point of his teaching, nor the Word, nor even the Word Incarnate taken in itself, it is the Word Incarnate as prolonged in that regenerate humanity which St Paul calls the "Body of Christ" (*Corpus Christi*: 1 Cor. 12. 27). This doctrine forms the substance of his *De incarnatione,* in which the following statements occur: "The Word was made man so that we should become gods", and this must be understood in a literal sense, "because we are in Christ as truly as the Word has entered into our nature since the Incarnation".

This thesis, which he had put forward even before his appointment as bishop, was developed in his *Discourse against the Arians* and it may be regarded as the very essence of his teaching. He affirms a close, even physical connection between the Incarnation of the Word and our deification. The proof of the divinity of the Incarnate Word lies in the fact that, by him, we are deified. In Jesus, the Word endows humanity with his divinity. "To this end he takes it upon himself with all its evils, but by the very fact that it is he who takes it he triumphs over them, for they had their origin only in separation from him." Men are closely linked to him: "In them as in him, thanks to that sharing in his life by reason of being 'part of the body of Jesus', incarnation and deification are united as two complementary aspects of a single reality." At the same time, "just as the Incarnation of the Word of Jesus and our deification in him are not only closely connected, but are, in-deed, fundamentally one and the same thing, so also are the Incarnation and the Redemption". The second and third homilies reinforce this doctrine. The general conclusion is very clear: the Church, the Body of Christ, provides the only valid explanation of the fact that (1) in Jesus the Word made man has "Wordified" us all, and (2) the Redemption is included in the Incarnation without in any sense being identical with it.

At the end of the fourth century, the Cappadocians carried on the work begun by the Patriarch of Alexandria. They went straight to the great mystery of the Trinity, not so much to sound its depths as to define it without ambiguity, since

Christian life depended on it. To restore the unity impaired by the secession of the Semi-Arians, numerous in the east in his time, St Basil adopted, and finally obtained acceptance for, the term hypostasis in the sense of person, in spite of the etymological meaning which rather suggests "substance". Thus he avoided Sabellian modalism which had been rife in the east and the potential danger of the word *persona* which could also lead to modalism. But, over and above these speculative questions, he was concerned with safeguarding the vital basis of religion, for all piety is fundamentally dependent on this mystery. Our sanctification is real only in so far as the "deification" which it implies is effected in and by a person who himself is truly God. He does not use the word "God" in order to avoid innovation: but it is implied of necessity in the whole of his treatise: the Son and the Holy Spirit are one God with the Father.

St Basil's brother, St Gregory of Nyssa, echoes him in his theories and still more so in his spiritual treatises, all of which are concerned with the great mystery. Their friend St Gregory Nazianzen sums up the thought of this great group of thinkers in his five admirable "discourses", called theological, but which, in fact, are Trinitarian; they point out how our Christian life is intensely bound up with the mystery of the God in three Persons. All religion hangs on this revelation which is prolonged in the sense that every Christian must endeavour to realize in his piety something of that divine reality which the mystery expresses.

In the fifth century, St Cyril of Alexandria was to do for the Word Incarnate what St Athanasius in the fourth did for the Trinity. Here we are faced with another aspect of the great Christian mystery. Already at the end of the fourth century, Apollinarius, an old friend of St Athanasius, dealt with it but came to grief by refusing to Christ a complete human soul, for fear of compromising his unity as a person: in his view a complete humanity would be a person. He was wrong: a complete humanity is a *nature*. The *person* is the possessor of that nature; and, in the case of Christ, the possessor is the Word who, in the Incarnation, assumed a complete human nature.

It was in his defence of this wholeness of Christ on the

human level that Nestorius, a rigid Antiochene, came to make too close a distinction between man and God in him, to the extent of maintaining that Mary was *mother of the man* but not "mother of God" (*Theotokos*). From Antioch he brought this doctrine to Constantinople, when he became bishop there in 428. By the end of that year a crisis had arisen and St Cyril, Patriarch of Alexandria and a distant successor of St Athanasius, immediately took his stand against Nestorius with letters to Egypt, Byzantium and Rome. The Pope empowered him to take action and, at Ephesus in 431, he approved, through his legates, the action taken by the saint right from the first sessions of the council. St Cyril was the providential defender of the unity of Christ as a person, a unity which is, in fact, the very basis of the Incarnation. He, more than anyone else, understood the meaning of this mystery and its supreme importance in the Christian life. At the same time, he was the embodiment of Catholicism in the east at a decisive period in the Church's history.

THE GREAT DOCTORS OF THE WEST

The fourth century in the west also produced wonderful contemplators of the great mysteries, notably St Hilary. He was to be the St Athanasius of the Latin world. Like him, he was a man of living faith and a fighter, rather than a speculative theologian. His great work on the Trinity is more than just a collection of scriptural texts; it is the testimony of a bishop exiled for the traditional faith and concerned, not only to defend it, but also to scrutinize its foundations, particularly the great mystery of God in Three Persons. From the time of his conversion, which he owed to St John's Prologue on the Word and the Incarnation (*De Trin.* 1. 10 *seq.*), he continued to be haunted by the great mystery of the Trinity, for he does not separate from the Father and the Son, the Holy Spirit who "receives" everything from the Son and so from the Father too. Is it not one and the same thing: to receive from the Son and to proceed from the Father? he asks: "All that the Holy Spirit receives, be it power or virtue or doctrine, the Son declares that the Holy Spirit receives it from him and he declares at the same time that he receives it also from the Father." But, for Hilary, this doctrine is not only a dogma of faith to be accepted on authority, it is a rule of life to be put into effect in one's conduct, by true Christian love. He had foreseen what the great Doctor of the west was later to expound with a fullness that is still unrivalled.

St Augustine surpassed all the Fathers of east and west alike by his sublime contemplation of the great mysteries, owing to the outstanding piety which inspired his vision.

Christ was no doubt its starting point, its support and its goal, but he was so, and could be so, only on account of his divine personality, for he is truly the Son of God, as well as Man-God, and King in the highest sense of the word.

The glimpse of God's nature granted to St Augustine when reading the *Hortensius* at the age of nineteen opened the eyes of his soul to the vision of a great ideal: but this was only a lightning flash in the storm. Ten years later, when the storm was past, he was granted further insights of a similar kind in Milan, partly through the discovery of Platonism, but still more through contact with true Christianity which presented itself, full of breadth and vitality, in the person of St Ambrose. Without neglecting the contributions of human wisdom, finally, at the age of thirty-two, he chose the God he found in his soul, both transcendent as Truth and present in him by grace.

The insistence on this twofold "indwelling" of God, one natural, the other supernatural, is perhaps the salient feature of St Augustine's teaching. The natural element is, of course, secondary; the essential, in his eyes, is of the supernatural order, a God who is one and transcendent, but in three Persons. The three have revealed themselves in turn: the Father by the Creation and the Old Testament; the Son by the Incarnation and the Redemption; the Holy Spirit by the Church and by the sanctity of the faithful on their journey to heaven. Only there will the City of God, in process of formation on earth, find its perfection.

St Augustine sees this mystery of the Holy Trinity for what it is, the highest point of Christian reality, extending beyond and above the highest plane of natural reality. But does this transcendent nature of the Holy Trinity not render it inaccessible to Man? Yes indeed, if by man we mean the natural man: but not when we enter the realm of faith. Faith is presented to us in terms which we understand, and by their means we can grasp many aspects of the mystery, even if we cannot reach the heart of it. The mission of the Doctors of the Church was precisely to express something of that mystery, so that souls might feed on it. St Augustine's was the foremost achievement in this respect, in his great work on the Trinity which, in a masterly fashion, crowns the efforts of several centuries. In the first seven books he makes a synthesis of all that is revealed on this subject, adding to it a theory of capital importance on *relation*, the basis of personality in God. In the next seven books (7–14) he endeavours to construct a series of illustrations of the great mystery, illustrations drawn from the outward and inward aspects of man, then rising from the sensual to the spiritual on the natural plane and finally to that divine or supernatural spirituality, which is perfect theological wisdom. The latter, which is the fruit of the gifts of the Holy Spirit, can bring about a very pure union with God in the prayer of the saints (Bk. 14, ch. 13, 15). It can also lead indirectly to a sublime knowledge of the great mystery; in Bk. 15, with an exposition of the loftiest aspects of this knowledge, St Augustine brings to a close his masterpiece of faith, prayer and wisdom.

While meditating on this great Christian dogma, St Augustine, in his struggle against Pelagius and his supporters, also endeavoured to fathom the mystery of grace on which this dogma depends. The basis of his teaching in this field is the lofty transcendence of God, which is such that we cannot reach him without some real condescension on his part, by divine adoption or cooperation: the former is a pure gift of God, the second is inconceivable without constant and effective support from him, foreseeing and sustaining all the actions of his creatures. This divine assistance is particularly necessary in the order of grace which, of its nature, is a gift of God for the purpose of sanctification and eternal life. Moreover, far from excluding the personal efforts of the creature, it solicits and sustains them. Men "are impelled to act, but this does not mean that the action is not their own", says Augustine. He calls the divine influence an "impulsion" rather than a movement; it is most efficacious (*efficacissima*), but suited to the subject (*congrua*) after a purely spiritual fashion and, like everything divine, profound in its effects, even more so than the delight which normally accompanies it but which is not inseparable from it. Grace, far from inhibiting freedom, actually increases it by bringing the soul closer to God, in whose image it is made, and towards whom it is striving.

This progress towards God is ensured and facilitated by sublime graces which St Augustine identifies with the seven gifts of the Holy Spirit, representing the highest modes of divine action in the souls of the saints: first, filial respect and piety; then strength and counsel; then knowledge and understanding; finally, crowning all, wisdom, the living synthesis of faith, hope and charity. The sublime action of the Holy Spirit is alone able to bring this about in souls submissive to grace and generous enough to answer all its calls. Such is the basis of the saint's teaching on the life of grace and on perfection. It finds its completion in an inner peace which foreshadows the life of eternity and even brings with it, for those souls who are generous and ready to be taught by the Spirit, a certain foretaste of its happiness. Those who talk of the pessimism of the saint, with reference to his doctrine of grace, clearly lay too much emphasis on secondary points at the expense of his fundamental theses, which are those of the best witnesses of the Christian life in the time of the Fathers. The Church's teaching on these matters has never wavered, though it may have been neglected by more recent teachers.

St Leo the Great (Pope 440–61) was appointed by Providence to put an authoritative end to the controversies raised, after the death of St Augustine, by the problem of grace, and particularly that of the personality of Christ, which arose when St Cyril of Alexandria denounced Nestorius' error to Pope St Celestine who had proceeded to condemn the idea of two persons in Christ. But certain formulas used by the Patriarch of Alexandria were abused, and a sort of monophysism, real or verbal, but in any case very dangerous, arose in the field of christology, denying or minimizing the human nature of our Saviour. The Pope intervened and, at the Council of Chalcedon, put forward, through his representatives, the doctrinal formula which was permanently accepted in the Church: "One and the same Christ, Son and Lord, only begotten Son in two natures without confusion, transformation, division or separation." St Leo, drawing abundant inspiration from St Augustine, was obliged to use certain formulas of a stronger kind than those used by the holy Doctor, in order to oppose new heresies threatening that greatest of all the Christian mysteries, the Incarnation of the Word. Christian piety was wholly dependent on it: Christ is not only God, but by his very nature he is unique. In his transcendent personality we find a miraculous blending of the immutable divine nature and a human nature created for the express purpose of establishing a permanent link between God and humanity, which in this world awaits that eternal life for which our earthly existence is a place of preparation ordained by Providence. This is the great Christian mystery, by which our human life is set in its true perspective on every level, and above all on that of eternal life. Such is the fundamental doctrine of which, from the beginning, the Fathers were the most ardent exponents.

CHAPTER V

TEACHERS OF THE

CHRISTIAN WAY OF LIFE

GREAT EDUCATORS

Here, the name of Clement of Alexandria immediately comes to mind. His apologia, the *Protreptica*, contains a tentative programme of ethical education addressed to the pagans in the hope of leading them to the Christian way of life. But the *Pedagogue* is still more suited to this purpose, as its title implies. Christ is the true educator of humanity and this title stands out above many others mentioned by the author, for, in his eyes, Jesus is also physician, general and pilot. Lofty as they are, these latter functions, though more than merely natural, are subordinate to the wisdom which Christ, the true Teacher, gives in person to those who follow him. This is the main theme of the second work of the Clementine Trilogy, and it deserves careful study, for it lays the foundations of a truly Christian education.

The *Stromata* sets out the principal laws of such an education, touching even on the most sublime aspects of it, with a breadth of vision astonishing for the author's time. Clement was a man of vast literary, philosophical and religious learning. He made abundant use of it all in this monumental study, the very title of which suggests the extent of the subjects treated and the variety of tones. Stromata means "tapestry", and the contents correspond to the title. A large number of classical allusions, drawn from the poets and philosophers of antiquity, are employed to raise the soul by gradual stages to an exalted spiritual life and a state of perfection which is described at all levels, though particularly at the highest. The seven Stromata have nothing in common with the seven Mansions of the Interior Castle later described by St Teresa, whose main preoccupation was with personal religious experience. In spite of occasional points of contact, Clement's approach is very different. Its main feature is faith, a faith so enlightened that he calls it knowledge (*gnosis*), the knowledge of divine things. This knowledge is closely linked with charity, and we must outline its characteristic features, for they were to have a strong influence on eastern theology as well as on eastern spirituality. We shall illustrate this point in the following chapter. For the moment, we may confine ourselves to a few observations on the subject of education that are closely connected with our theme.

"Gnosis", which for Clement is the ideal of any Christian education on a somewhat advanced level, is the synthesis of religious culture informed by charity, in accordance with St Paul's exhortation (the Apostle recommends to the Galatians "the faith that finds its expression in love") and a certain natural culture, particularly in philosophy, which cannot itself attain perfection, even on the human plane, without supernatural assistance. This profound, and in certain respects, inspired vision of the harmonious relation between the two orders, human and divine, and even of a certain relative necessity for their union, was too novel not to meet with resistance, nor was the author yet in a position to expound it with the necessary subtlety, which was to be achieved only after centuries of searching and hesitation. His thought was nonetheless valuable and it was to stimulate the greatest minds in their search for a lofty culture, moral and religious as well as doctrinal and intellectual. It contained the germ of Alexandrine spirituality.

Origen carried on the work begun by Clement and gave it a more clearly religious tone. Born shortly after 180, he was too young when his master left Alexandria in 201, to have received more than a groundwork of instruction from him. This left its mark, but it was broad enough also to leave scope for its own personality. He was a man of powerful originality, even more so, perhaps, than his brilliant precursor. He was fundamentally a man of prayer as well as a scholar, and above all he was an exegete, dedicated to meditation on the Scriptures. His thought was dominated by the supernatural as manifested in the Scriptures and he penetrated their treasures to the point of mysticism. In his efforts to interpret the Scriptures, he sought determinedly for the spirit hidden behind the letter and his purpose was to form perfect Christians. Following the example of his master, he was a great educator, but in a Christian manner in which faith plays an even more important part than with Clement. He exercised his mind on the word of God as contained in the sacred books, but he cannot be called a pure exegete, even in the spiritual sense. His desire is to form complete Christians in the highest sense of the word, not simply natural men, but men who are Christians before all else, and his ideal implies a true mysticism. His *gnosis* is indeed similar to that of his master, with possibly a more markedly divine character.

"Origenism" is characterized by the love of Scripture and above all by the searching for the spiritual meaning behind it. This spiritual meaning is reached by a use of allegory so determined as to be characteristic. Origenism became synonymous with allegorism. But to this must be added a particular feature, namely, his emphasis on the *spiritual life* realized in the members of the Church in whom, since Pentecost, Christ lives on in this world. This mysticism, which is an infinite extension of the biblical types shown in the Scriptures, is founded on a wide appeal to the gifts of the Holy Spirit. In this field Origen had precursors: St Justin, St Irenaeus and Clement; but he surpasses them all by the use he makes of those gifts in expounding the perfect Christian life.

After these two outstanding masters of a higher Christian life, whose impact was as beneficial as it was decisive, in spite of a certain incompleteness in their thought, we need mention only a few other remarkable spiritual guides for chosen souls in quest of perfection in those days of Christian antiquity. In their own way, they were educators in the broad sense of the word, making use of Holy Scripture rather than of human knowledge in the manner of the official Pedagogues.

Beside them we may perhaps place St Cyprian (210–58), as a Christian teacher in Latin Africa, where his fame flourished in the third century, leaving a deep imprint in spite of his swift passage. Most of his writings may be classified in this category, even the four short apologetic works, in two of which he is mainly concerned with ethical questions. This is still truer of another series of "Opuscula", especially those based on Tertullian from whom he covertly drew his inspiration, skilfully toning down their excesses and thus preparing in advance for the re-entry into Catholic life of this great man's writings. Centuries were to pass before this took place, but it is now an accomplished fact, thanks partly to Cyprian. He lacked Tertullian's genius, but he was, above all, a man of stability and judgement, primary qualities of all true educators. This, added to the glory of his martyrdom, makes him, without doubt, the greater of the two.

We might quote great names from the fourth century, but they are best dealt with elsewhere, in view of the general character of their activity in the ancient world. A few stand out, however, especially in the east, namely, the three Cappadocians, St Basil, St Gregory Nazianzen and St Gregory of Nyssa, men of lofty culture, differing greatly indeed, but united in spiritual brotherhood, even more than by family ties (the second Gregory was a younger brother of Basil). The first two mentioned had a strong appreciation of the value of classical culture, and St Basil, in a famous text, insists on its usefulness, not merely on the aesthetic plane, but also for moral formation and the understanding of the Scriptures themselves in this respect (Homily 22). A few years later, in the neighbouring province of Antioch, St John Chrysostom said the same thing, and his example was more effective than his theories. At the same time, in the Latin west, Providence raised up imitators of a high quality in St Ambrose, St Augustine and above all St Jerome, who to the end attached the highest importance to literary form, without prejudice to the teaching it contained. Most of these men were preachers, and we must particularly bear in mind this aspect of their work: care for their flock takes first place, not only in the teaching of the Fathers but in all their preaching.

CATECHISTS AND PREACHERS OF THE EAST

The greatest of all the eastern catechists of early Christian times is St Cyril of Jerusalem. It is true that his contemporary, St Gregory of Nyssa, wrote a *Catechesis* which is famous, but it is a summary of the Christian religion rather than a call to the life of prayer. This is achieved only in part in the "Sacramentary" of Serapion, Bishop of Thmuis in Egypt (fourth century), a collection of prayers of which he is perhaps not the only author and which in any case only contains some formal prayers referring to the sacred rites. Though not without value, they are inadequate. On the other hand, the *Catecheses* of St Cyril (313–86), Bishop of Jerusalem, comprises a complete account of those points of doctrine which serve as the foundation for the Christian life. The articles of faith contained in the creed (4–18) are by no means divorced from their moral applications; similarly the study of the rites which provides the framework of these accounts (1–3 and 19–23) is far from being a merely speculative one. (Modern criticism attributes the last mentioned to a successor of Cyril of Jerusalem, by the name of John, who certainly preached and wrote towards the end of the fourth century.) It is true that he warns the neophytes against the contemporary errors of the pagans, Jews, Samaritans, heretics and Manichees. But what strikes us most on reading these pages is the life of faith which speaks in them with such compelling tones. He is the greatest witness to Palestinian piety in the fourth century.

St Ephrem (†373), greatest of the Syrian Doctors, was a simple deacon but a great preacher too, and a poet of inexhaustible fertility. For the last ten years of his life he was a refugee from Persia in Edessa (north-east of Syria), where he represents pure traditional Catholicism, prior to the deviations caused by the christological factions in the following century: for centuries Nestorians and Monophysites were to quarrel over the remnants of this unhappy corner of Christendom. For all, St Ephrem is a link with the Catholic Church, remaining its purest glory as a moralist and ascetic, and even more so as a mystic, piously devoted to Christ, the Man-God, to his Mother

Mary and to the Church as Mystical Bride, which are the main aspects of his very living and practical theology. In spite of its profusion, his work had great value thanks to its penetrating teaching and fervent piety.

St John Chrysostom, also a Syrian, but of the west, an Antiochene of noble family and great learning, was the supreme master of Christian preaching in the east and throughout the Empire. To a comprehensive knowledge of Greek culture he added, on the one hand, several years of solitude spent in the mountains near Antioch and, on the other, his study of the Scriptures, both the Old and the New Testaments, and above all St Paul, who helped him to grasp their deeper meaning. His *Treatise on the Priesthood,* in which, as a young man, he sums up his ideas on pastoral activity and particularly on preaching, shows that he had meditated at length on its fundamental principles: he always regards prayer and study as the basis of the Christian apostolate. To overlook this would be to distort his teaching. There is, however, a double stumbling-block to be avoided. On the one hand, we must take care not to think that, because he is an Antiochene, the saint is primarily a scholar, nor must we regard him as a speculative theologian because he belongs to the east. In point of fact, he had an acute sense of doctrine; on occasion he was to confound the Arian philosophers whose quibblings were so detrimental to faith. On the other hand, it would be equally unjust to regard him as being so much a man of action as to be a merely empirical guide devoid of all doctrinal insight. Clearly St John Chrysostom has an acute awareness of the importance of ethics, but it is founded on a profound and living belief. He was a great disciple of St Paul, and his commentaries, always clear and compelling, are incomparable calls to the life of faith. It is true that he often states or implies that God is ineffable and incomprehensible, a view which leads to respectful adoration rather than loving intimacy. In his case, worship is connected with a general sense of the grandeur of God who is the object of wonder as much as of love. It is accompanied by amazement, anguish, dizziness, fear, trembling, terror, all terms which the saint frequently employs. The divine nature which he preaches has nothing abstract about it: it is situated far above created things, truly transcendent and yet "experienced as a presence of terrible reality".

But this tendency is balanced by other qualities on which the preacher of Antioch lays equal emphasis, particularly justice and kindness; he speaks of these virtues with great warmth and poetic feeling and stoutly defends them against the Manichees. The Pauline doctrine of grace is less marked than in the case of Augustine, but it is clear enough, and he even distinguishes between the two wills in God with regard to sinners: one, that they should not perish (*first will*), the other that they should be punished (*second will*).

This great master of the Christian life was bound to lay emphasis on the sacramental rites, and indeed he freely recommends the most important of them, especially the Eucharist, which holds a large place in his work. He has even been called the "Doctor of the Eucharist". In this field, his realism is bold, almost exaggerated: "Not only are we about to see our Saviour, we shall also take him in our hands, eat him, crush him with our teeth, become united to him in the most intimate manner. . . . All that our Saviour did not suffer on the Cross (for instance, the breaking of a single bone) he suffers it today for love of us, and allows himself to be broken into crumbs so that we may all be filled." He goes much farther in his catechesis than St Cyril of Jerusalem or even St Gregory of Nyssa. In these texts the preacher aims less at explaining the mystery than at stirring up the faithful, already familiar with the ordinary teaching.

From the fifth century onwards, the Byzantine Church cultivated the homily more than the catechesis; we might point out particularly the Marian homilies, of which many new texts have been published in the twentieth century. They testify to real progress in devotion to the Mother of God: her Immaculate Conception and her Assumption are clearly taught though usually by implication. Among the most prominent preachers in this field we must mention those of the eighth century, and particularly St Germanus, Patriarch of Constantinople, St Andrew of Crete, Metropolitan of Gortyna, St John Damascene, a priest of Jerusalem, the last Doctor of the Eastern

Church, and a staunch defender of the veneration of images and devotion to our Lady.

At the end of the eighth century and the beginning of the ninth a great Byzantine monk, St Theodore the Studite, repeats in loftier catechetical form the teaching of those we have just mentioned, for his *Smaller* and *Greater Catecheses* were addressed to a select group of religious. Less preoccupied with doctrine than the others, and anxious mainly to foster spiritual growth, first of all in the monks, but also in the faithful who at that time maintained close contact with them, his work reflects at length the Christian life of Byzantium, on the eve of the schism which was to take place there, to the detriment of that full catholicity which was once the glory of the Eastern Church.

PREACHERS AND PASTORS OF THE WEST

The outstanding master of theoretical and practical catechesis in the Latin world is still St Augustine. He may be considered as the western counterpart to St John Chrysostom, whom he piously emulated without actually imitating him. He wrote on the training of neophytes (*De Catechizandis rudibus*), having previously, in the first book of his *Christian Doctrine*, dealt in a more general manner with the method of preaching the Word of God. For him eloquence is of secondary importance; what matters is a living faith in the God in Three Persons, who abandons his lofty transcendence to give himself to us in creation, in his redeeming Incarnation and in the Church indwelt by the Holy Spirit, provided that we live in charity, the laws of which Augustine sets out at the beginning of the same work. The following three books supplement it in various ways, but St Augustine's many sermons provide the best commentary on it. We can confine ourselves to general outlines.

The source of Augustine's doctrine must often be sought in the Old Testament, which provided him with texts for fifty sermons and particularly for his 200 homilies on the Psalms (*Enarrationes*). For the most part these are true commentaries on the Christian life and, perhaps, the finest of all his sermons.

More readable, however, are the homilies on St John (*Tractatus*: 124 on the Gospel and 10 on the 1st Epistle). As well as these, he wrote more than 500 sermons on particular subjects, on the Old and New Testaments (nearly 150), on the liturgy and the saints, and on many other doctrinal themes.

The keynote of Augustine's sermons is his emphasis on faith as a life-principle. For this Doctor, the great source of all education is faith, that is, the Holy Trinity, Christ and the Church in all its aspects. In other words, it is theology as understood by the ancient writers, less concerned with speculative research than with its practical application. For him, progress in piety is inseparable from dogmatic belief, and particularly from faith in Christ living in the Church. His commentaries on the Old Testament psalms are most illuminating in this respect, and even more so are his treatises on St John, that most doctrinal of all the Gospels, with its perfect combination of speculation and moral purpose, of asceticism and pure and lofty mysticism, based on the surest supernatural knowledge.

One theme stands out in all these pastoral writings: *the love of God*. Of all the titles given to St Augustine, the most important, and certainly the most popular, is that of Doctor of Charity, usually symbolized by a heart crowned with flames. The theme of charity has constantly recurred in the preceding summaries of doctrine. It will become still more prominent when we come to speak of ethics, of which it is the very soul, both in respect of those general rules which properly speaking are the object of ethics and of those special methods which tend towards perfection (asceticism), and most of all in respect of those higher gifts granted to complete the work of perfection (mysticism). The latter is the most important of the three, and we shall come back to it in the next chapter.

In spite of the greatness of St Augustine, we must not forget those other great pastors of the west who were mighty exponents of the Christian life.

The best known, and undoubtedly the greatest of them, was St Ambrose. He was St Augustine's father in the faith. Such was the impression made by Ambrose's public teaching on the sceptical and defiant young rhetorician, who arrived in Milan in 384, that, two years later, Augustine was a changed man, thanks largely to these words full of light and strength, striking at the heart of the great doctrinal and moral problems with which he was obsessed. Ambrose was, first and foremost, a man of action and a moralist. He was not impervious to philosophy, particularly that of Plotinus, who seemed to have given wings to that Stoicism which reigned in the educated Roman circles of the period. He was also attracted by Origen's oriental speculation. But he always emphasized the moral aspect, most suited to his character and his mission, for his providentially allotted rôle seems to have been to provide the west with the sure and living teaching which it needed so greatly at this period of transition. Thus he prepared the way for St Augustine, who was to develop his work and render it permanent, by extending it to every field, on the eve of the great cataclysm which was soon to overwhelm the centre of the Empire.

In the following century and in the same part of the world, but speaking from a more eminent position, St Leo the Great represents the highest form of Christian dogmatic teaching, namely that given by the supreme Pastor: for the hundred or so surviving sermons of this great pontiff are all directly aimed at enriching and strengthening the faith of his flock, urging them to asceticism (fasting), extolling the Christian mysteries, reminding them of the privileges of the Roman Church whose mission, as the successor of St Peter, is to rule in the name of Christ.

The life and Passion of our Saviour provide the usual basis for his doctrinal works, which are those of a pastor rather than of a speculative theologian. He is instinctively drawn towards ethical subjects. Many pages might be quoted on the examination of conscience, the Devil, concupiscence, prayer, faith and charity, those two wings on which the Christian is borne to heaven (sermon 45, 2), and on spiritual childhood (sermon 37, 3). Grace is not forgotten, and he speaks of it frequently in the manner of St Augustine, but carefully pointing out the need to cooperate with grace, to love and seek for him who first of all loved and sought for us. His zeal is often expressed in urgent exhortations to struggle against the passions, and to perform all our actions for the love of God. He formulated the great law of progress so often repeated by spiritual directors: "Not to advance is to lose ground, and to gain nothing is to lose something." (*Qui non proficit deficit et qui non acquirit, non nihil perdit.*)

We must also mention two preachers, contemporaries of St Leo, whose eloquence reflected honour on the Church in Italy: namely, St Peter Chrysologus who has left 176 sermons and St Maximus of Turin who has left close on 270. But the best known of all those, between St Leo and St Gregory the Great, who exerted great pastoral influence was St Caesarius of Arles who for forty years (503–43) was bishop of the primatial see of south Gaul. Though not much of a speculative theologian, he was an organizer and a man of action. He was largely inspired by St Augustine, particularly in his sermons in which he frequently quotes the great African Doctor word for word; hence many mistakes on the part of the first editors. His style, though not incorrect, is extremely simple; the preacher does not hesitate to use rustic expressions, so that, as he explains, "the Lord's flock may receive the heavenly food in plain and simple language, and, since the ignorant cannot rise to the level of scholars, the scholars must condescend to the ignorance of their brethren". His sermons on the mysteries and his homilies on Scripture are more elevated in tone, but the greater part of his preaching is of a markedly practical character.

St Gregory the Great (540–604) was, for his time, a distant echo of the great voices of St Augustine and St Leo the Great, distant in every respect indeed, but how clear in spite of the chaos which reigned in Italy and throughout the west in his time. Doctrinally he is inspired by St Augustine, as regards those points of doctrine which, in such a time of darkness, were calculated to cast light on the great dogmatic truths on which traditional Christian morality, with all its demands, is based. He emphasized not only the basic teachings but also those tending towards a lofty spiritual idea. In the fourteen years of his episcopate (590–604), his mission seems, on the other hand, to have been that of presenting this Christian ideal in such a manner as to make it available to the whole Church, not only in the west where she was striving to convert the barbarians, but also in the Imperial east, handicapped by ever-increasing

State control. In both fields St Gregory was a true teacher of an intensive Christian life, as far as was possible in his time.

His preaching, known to us through some sixty homilies on various texts from Ezechiel and the Gospels, shows the desire of the recently elected pope to instruct and enlighten his flock as a whole. This spiritual purpose is even more clearly defined in the *Moralia*, a vast treatise on asceticism and mysticism, based on the book of Job, but inspired in fact by the experience of the saints and his own apostolic zeal. Facts and quotations are always chosen with a view to practical application, aimed at leading generous souls to that true contemplation in which God shows himself to the soul, inspiring in it the purest love and ever-increasing willingness in his service. By his writings, St Gregory did much to encourage men to strive after the life of perfection, both among the clergy, to whom his *Regula Pastoralis* is specially addressed, and among the monks whom he groups as far as possible around St Benedict, to whom he devotes a whole book of his popular *Dialogues*. All this activity, while leaving room for his purely administrative work, and seeming even to stimulate and sustain it, is a wonderful example of what St Paul calls "that faith which finds expression in love" (Gal. 5. 6), and which seems to have been the guiding rule of his life. This above all makes him a faithful witness to the patristic tradition of his time.

In Italy too, shortly before St Gregory's time, we have Cassiodorus, who shared the fame of Boethius at the court of Theodoric, and outlasted him there. He was a sort of Minister for Internal Affairs, a learned historian and a great educator of the Goths who had established themselves on the ruins of the Empire. In 540, at the age of sixty, he retired to a monastery founded by himself and, until his death in 570, continued his work as educator to the barbarians occupying Italy. He died in the odour of sanctity, and yet he has never been the object of a real cultus as Boethius was at Pavia. He appears as a scholar rather than a saint. He resembles Boethius in his love of letters, but differs from him in every other respect. Whereas Boethius is a philosopher and a speculative theologian Cassiodorus is primarily a practical man. He is less concerned with ideas than with intellectual and moral education and to this end he makes use of the ancient pagan authors as well as of ecclesiastical works. He frequently quoted both, and the services he thus rendered to medieval culture were immense.

St Isidore, Archbishop of Seville (†636), is undoubtedly the greatest Spanish writer of early times. He exerted a decisive national influence on the councils. These had a religious and political character, the latter usually inspired by the former. He did a great deal to revive learning after the occupation of the country by its new inhabitants. A tireless writer, his numerous works, some of which have a positively encyclopedic character, deal with every possible subject. Many of them are devoted to the Scriptures, history, the Church. He is more of a scholar than an original thinker; yet, even in this respect, his importance was considerable and he was one of the great educators of the Middle Ages. All his knowledge came from the past; he added nothing to it. From St Augustine and St Gregory he borrowed his theological and ascetical teaching and he delved deeply into the treasures of ancient literature. Moreover, he was remarkably gifted as a compiler, and is perhaps the greatest the world has ever seen. He combined a broad intelligence and an unerring memory with great facility of clear and rapid expression; and although his language is corrupted by the intrusion of many foreign words, his definitions are often astonishingly precise. He earned the title of Doctor of the Church.

In England, in the following century, St Bede won the same title, but on very different grounds. Apart from a few didactic writings, his work is entirely religious. This applies even to his history of the English nation, but principally to his commentaries on the Old and New Testaments, for he explained nearly all of them and his writings were widely read. Thus, he was a true promoter of Christian life, both inside and outside the monasteries. He is often a faithful echo of St Augustine and St Jerome and, in this way, his work is extremely valuable. In other respects he is more original, but concerned with mystical applications rather than with theological speculation. This reduces his value for our time, whereas it brought the Middle Ages to his feet. He is the last of the great Doctors of the West.

CHAPTER VI

MYSTICS AND MASTERS OF THE SPIRITUAL LIFE: INTIMACY WITH GOD

THE FIRST CHRISTIAN MYSTICS

Strictly speaking, the term mystic is applied only to those Christians for whom baptism is the basis of a real intimacy with God, present in them by sanctifying grace. This intimacy is the characteristic element in all true mysticism. As well as faith in the Three Persons, it implies a close union with them through acts of hope and charity so intense as to make possible a certain experience of their presence. Such acts, which are the fruit of grace and the cooperation of each individual with its promptings, are particularly attributed to the Holy Spirit living in those who have been baptized in the name of Christ. These basic features of mysticism are already implicit in the Epistle of St Clement of Rome, but they stand out forcibly in those of St Ignatius of Antioch. We have already mentioned the main texts of this author at the beginning of this work, so eloquent are they as regards this characteristic trait of the Fathers.

St Irenaeus lacks the fire of St Ignatius, but his work, full of warmth and learning, bears ample witness to his ideal of the Christian life. In his teaching, as in that of St Paul, great emphasis is placed on the Holy Spirit. For him, the baptized Christian is made up of three parts, body, soul and spirit. This last term denotes both the higher part of the soul and the Holy

Spirit himself, who habitually dwells in every Christian submissive to his action. The perfecting of man, which begins at the first outpouring of the Holy Spirit and is completed only in heaven, is already a reality in this world through the harmonious unity of the three elements, when a man opens his heart to the Holy Spirit and obeys his promptings. In this world the life of the Spirit must also find expression in intellectual effort. Every Christian formed in the school of the Spirit will be able to pass judgement in all things. He will see clearly the folly of pagan and heretic. He will adhere with all his heart to God, to Jesus Christ and to his Church. He will recognize in the life of the Incarnate Word the fulfilment of those prophecies inspired by the Spirit; he will recognize the Spirit's action in those present generations which have to be won for the Word.

For Irenaeus, this sublime teaching was the spiritual basis of a gradual assimilation of man to God. To it he added a less well-founded theory of the millennium which the Church of his time had not yet condemned, but which did not prejudice his work as a whole.

Much more dangerous was the heresy of Montanism, which proclaimed a new divine incarnation, allegedly realized in the person of Montanus of Phrygia at the end of the second century. This illuminism went hand in hand with a very grave heresy. The bishops of Asia intervened and were supported by the popes. Those "enlightened ones" had partisans in Rome itself, and St Victor was obliged to oppose them. They made proselytes as far away as Africa, and Tertullian was won over to their side. He died an unrepentant member of the sect, so greatly was he dazzled by this false mysticism. The downfall of Tertullian is all the sadder since this brilliant apologist and powerful controversialist seemed destined by his gifts for influential activity in a wider sphere. He cut himself off in his rebellion, and died in obscurity at an advanced age. The decade of unadulterated Catholicism, which had followed his conversion in about 195, was fertile in works of great value. One of them is devoted to prayer and contains one of the earliest known commentaries on the Lord's Prayer. St Cyprian later drew inspiration from it in his own short treatise on "the Lord's prayer" (*De oratione dominica*).

This theme of prayer is one of those which recur most frequently in early spiritual writings, and in this respect the most learned of the Fathers resembles the simple pastors. In spite of apparent differences between the ordinary faithful and more learned Christians, there was always real spiritual communion between all true members of the Church. The *Didache*, a popular work of unknown authorship which is perhaps the oldest patristic document, and the *Apostolic Tradition* of St Hippolytus (early third century) lay great emphasis on public prayer in common, making it clear that the Christian is united to God in and through a society; but this does not exclude private prayer which is also mentioned, at least incidentally, at the end of the treatise.

The author of the third century who wrote most deeply on prayer was the great Alexandrine exegete, Origen, a mystical writer in the highest sense of the word. His homilies show that, for him, prayer implies a real personal intimacy with the Christian God in Three Persons. He delights in finding prophetic references in the Old Testament and manifestations of it in the New, through Christ and the Holy Spirit. The gaps in his theology of the Trinity are compensated for by the intuitive knowledge derived from his contemplative life. He sets out the basic rules of this life in an excellent general work on prayer. He begins by explaining the general teaching on the subject, and completes it with a detailed commentary on the Lord's Prayer. But his innumerable commentaries on Holy Scripture and his homilies clearly show the mystical tendency of his thought which scarcely considers the letter of Scripture and even sweeps past its ethical significance in order to arrive at the contemplation of the divine mysteries on which it dwells, by a sort of higher instinct which is both the sign and the fruit of his contemplation. He may have exaggerated at times, but we cannot deny the value of the principle and the excellence with which, on the whole, he applied it. In him, Christian mysticism becomes fully aware of its true source, the divinely inspired writings, and of its mission, which is to lead to the perfect life those Christians who are submissive to the Holy Spirit.

THE MYSTICS OF THE GREAT CENTURY IN THE EAST

At every stage in this Great Century, which we must consider as including 150 years of intense Christian activity, we find real men of prayer. These may be grouped around two Doctors, as outstanding in this respect as in all others—St John Chrysostom in the east and St Augustine in the west. The brilliance of their spiritual activity, situated at the centre of the period in question, must not cause us to forget their precursors and those who continued their work.

St Athanasius, that living symbol of the Nicaean faith in the fourth century, was a man of prayer in the highest sense as well as a fighter, and his friendship with St Antony, whose life he wrote, is at least a sign if not actually a proof of this. The proof is to be found in the manner in which he fought his doctrinal battle for the divinity of Christ, for that is what was at stake and with it the whole of Christianity. Those who denied it were philosophers, fervent disciples of Plato or Aristotle, Zeno or Plotinus. Far from following them in their sophisms, Athanasius knows only one book, the Bible, only one master, the Holy Spirit, only one guide, the Church (see above, ch. IV). But all this becomes a living reality only by the action of grace, in prayer. For Athanasius, the names of Father, Son and Holy Spirit are not mere words or even pure ideas; they are true and lofty realities, tangible and alive, in which God lives and through which we live in God. At the very sound of these words his whole being vibrates with religious fervour. This fervour derives from his profound realization of our close union in love with these divine realities, since God condescends to draw us by grace into their transcendent life, in the Word which was made flesh so that we might become the children of God, as St John puts it.

For Athanasius this is no mere doctrinal truth to be accepted by the intellect; it is a reality lived and experienced in prayer. And this experience is, as it were, the living synthesis of the two wisdoms: Eternal Wisdom which stoops to us in grace and a created wisdom which is the Christian's response to the

gift of God. It is as a pure mystic that Athanasius replies to the
heretics of his time: "God does not need us: he has life in
himself, in the eternal generation of the Son. But, of his own
free will God draws us so near to him as to bring us into the
intimacy of his own life. Not only has he created us simply to
be united to his only Son, but, contemplating him in eternity,
he contemplates us in this union which must be accomplished
in time, so that he no longer sees him as separated from us. In
the perfect vision of things which the Father has, Divine Wisdom and created Wisdom are not merged as the Arians would
have it, but they are espoused." (L. Bouyer, *L'Incarnation et
l'Église,* p. 145.)

The Cappadocians who carried on St Athanasius' doctrinal
struggle against the Arians, did not, however, press it from
the same mystical point of view. They intervened particularly
on behalf of the Holy Spirit and emphasized his deifying action,
an action which presupposes the true divinity of its author.
St Gregory of Nyssa, the brother of St Basil and the most
mystically inclined of the three Doctors in this group, has
described in various ways the stages by which the soul ascends
towards God, present in it by grace. It was left to St Augustine
to carry on St Athanasius' teaching on the union of the Divine
Persons among themselves, which is the basis of mystical knowledge in the Church. The Bishop of Nyssa is more attracted
by the psychological aspect of the ascent of the soul towards
God. He likes to base his teaching on the Old Testament: the
"Life of Moses", for instance, provides him with material for
a classification of the spiritual ways in three stages: the Burn-
ing Bush represents the soul's setting out; the Cloud, the
spiritual progress towards contemplation; the Darkness on
Sinaï, the summits of the mystical life. In his homilies on the
Psalms, Ecclesiastes and the Song of Songs, the saint develops
this theme, covering the same ground. The same teaching is
continued in the eight homilies on the Beatitudes and the five
devoted to the Lord's Prayer. These instances clearly show the
author's tendency: he was to become one of the masters of
mysticism in the east, together with the "Areopagite" whom
he anticipates by his borrowings from the philosophers. He
seems to have been particularly familiar with Plotinus, but his

deepest inspiration comes from Scripture. He is more a Christian than a philosopher, whatever may have been said about him in this respect. His influence on the east was considerable, particularly in Byzantium, where he profited by the unrivalled prestige of his friend, St Gregory Nazianzen, with whom he was often confused.

St John Chrysostom, the glory of the Church of Antioch, was less drawn to mysticism than the masters of Alexandria or even those of Cappadocia, although there are clear traces of it in many of his works. His apostolate was pre-eminently that of a practical preacher and moralist, but he was sustained by a lofty idea of God which gave unity to his life and great power to his preaching. But this living idea of God, this "theology", was the fruit of years of solitary life devoted to prayer and meditation on the Scriptures, and particularly his favourite author, St Paul. In all his writings he appealed to the power and wisdom of God, his mercy and his love; he proclaimed his justice and his will and magnificently defended his rights. Perhaps the finest of his sermons were inspired by the thought of the greatness of God and the fragility of his creatures, examples of which are to be found in the homilies on the fall of Eutropius. His sense of the vanity of the things of this world, so forcefully expressed in them, necessarily implies a clear realization that God is all: God is the port which knows no storm, the true city, far from which we are but travellers, dwelling in an inn for a day and passing on.

St Cyril of Alexandria at the beginning of the fifth century also exhibits, in his own way, a clearly mystical trend, and this was perhaps the secret of his strength in the struggle against Nestorian dualism. This heresy struck at the very heart of Christianity. What St Athanasius in the fourth century had done to defend the divinity of the Word as a Person, even independently of his Incarnation, his successor in the fifth century did to uphold the unity of this Person of the Word even in his Incarnation. He was guided by the doctrinal tradition of his Church, and also by that of the Alexandrine School which always gave first place in its doctrinal speculations to the principles touching the Divine Nature, regarded not only from the point of view of its natural rights but even in its sublime personal relations. A certain tradition of mysticism, which had existed in Alexandria since the time of Origen, led the theologians of that Church to keep the Divine Nature and even the Divine Persons in the foreground of their thought. The highest gifts of the Holy Spirit enable the perfect Christian to realize this in his life of piety, and thinkers, especially mystics, can benefit from it in their writings. Are we to attribute such gifts to St Cyril? We cannot in any case deny them on the grounds of his violent resistance to Nestorius, for this very violence may well have issued from lofty inspiration; its providential effect is too often overlooked by certain historians.

THE MYSTICS OF THE GREAT CENTURY IN THE WEST

Once again we shall confine ourselves to two outstanding personalities, St Ambrose and St Augustine. They met in this life and their mysticism also formed a point of contact in spite of their differences in this respect, as in many others.

St Ambrose, the son of a Prefect of the Roman Empire, was a counsellor to the Emperors at the end of the fourth century; he is often known only by the part that as a Churchman he played in politics; but, great as it was, this rôle remained subordinate to that of pastor, moralist and educator of the Christian people and that of ascetic leading souls into the way of perfection. This latter function is extremely prominent and includes a strong mystical tendency. It stands out clearly in his writings on virginity, which he praised more than any writer of his time. He compares it to a true "marriage with Christ", a marriage which imposes duties but which brings with it many privileges. These are of an entirely spiritual nature, for virginity is a gift of God and its home is heaven. Its unrivalled model is Mary, who remains its foundress and its perfect ideal to the end of time. This is the theme of the most moving of his four treatises on the subject, that entitled "The Training of a Virgin" (De institutione virginis, written about 392).

But the true criterion of the saint's mysticism is that lofty union with God on which it is founded. This manifests itself particularly in his sense of the presence of God in the Christian soul and in his manner of describing it in one of the first

treatises on virginity: "We possess all things in Christ," he
says. "Have you a wound to be healed? He is the physician.
Do you burn with fever? He is the fountain. Are you overwhelmed with injustice? He is justice. Do you seek assistance?
He is strength. Do you fear death? He is Life. Do you long
for heaven? He is the way. Do you flee from darkness? He is
Light. Are you hungry? He is food. Taste then, and see how
good the Lord is. Blessed is the man who hopes in him"
(16. 96). Christ is the source of all virtue. In a letter to Felix,
the bishop whom he consecrated, he gives a moving description
of the treasures of the Christian sanctuary where, together with
the Scriptures containing the teaching of wisdom, is to be found
the holy tabernacle where Christ dwells, speaking to us and
fulfilling all our needs. ("Where Christ is, there all things are
to be found.") Ambrose goes even farther: spiritual gifts come
from him alone; peace and justice are a sign of the presence
of Christ. ("Where peace is found, there is Christ.") Christ
dwells in the soul; nay more, he goes forward in it, through
his Spirit and his sanctifying action. He who receives him and
recognizes him with love, places, as it were, a pious kiss at his
feet. The freshness of feeling, reminiscent of St Bernard, sur-
prises us in the grave counsellor who had the ear of the
Emperors of the great Christian Century. It is normal in a
mystic whose soul is fixed in God, whatever his worldly preoccupations. We shall find the same note ringing out even more
clearly in the case of the Bishop of Hippo.

The writings of St Augustine in the west contain the most
complete and most profound teaching on mysticism to be found
in all antiquity. It is a pure echo of that of St Paul and St
John, whence its character is derived. In spite of certain
appearances, philosophy is clearly subordinated to the supernatural. The excitement which St Augustine felt when at the
age of nineteen he discovered wisdom through his reading of
Cicero's *Hortensius* was more philosophical than religious, but
religion played its part in it. It comes to the fore in his *Fecisti
nos ad te!* at the beginning of the Confessions, written at the
age of forty-two: "Thou hast made us for thyself and our
hearts are restless till they rest in thee!" It was after his conversion at the age of thirty-two that Augustine had his first

real experience of this peace. For the first call of wisdom before
his twentieth year had not borne fruit until much later.

The young man was immediately led astray by his adherence to the Manichaean sect which taught a brutal opposition
between good and evil, forces eternally in conflict in each one
of us. He remained a member for ten years. He was rescued
from this error towards the age of thirty by his study of Neo-
Platonism, which taught him the predominance of a single
principle, essentially good, in which the Word played a prominent part. But this philosophy, lofty and pure as it was or
claimed to be on the moral and religious plane, seemed very
arid to him. All his life he was to make use of its principles;
but he was profoundly and bitterly aware of its deficiencies in
the religious, moral and spiritual sphere. For him all this is
closely bound up with the Man-God.

Augustine never forgot his mother's early lessons in devotion
to Christ. Yet it was towards the age of thirty, when entering
on his great period of religious maturity, that he became fully
aware of its importance. It sustained him in his revolt against
the arid speculations of Platonism which might have been his
downfall. It was above all St Paul who brought him true enlightenment on the mysteries of Christianity: the mystery of
sin which is death and that of grace which is life, the life of
God within us, received in baptism and fostered by the action
of the Holy Spirit. This is the only force which can snatch us
from the exile of sin and lead us to that land where God
awaits us.

For him, the Apostle Paul was to remain the true master
who enabled him to explore the depths of Christianity. Having
rescued him from sin, he taught him to live in union with God
by that ardent and light-giving charity of which the Holy Spirit
is the source and sustainer. This teaching blossomed into contemplation of the Word, as revealed step by step in the writings
of St John. Augustine's commentaries on him show that,
together with St Paul, his favourite master is the disciple whom
Jesus loved.

The outstanding feature of Augustine's piety is its spirituality. He sees God as present in man: *intimus cordi est!* And
this is true even on the natural plane, for he loves to ascend

by reasoned steps through the life of the mind to the Creator. But this philosophical approach, although true and profound, does not satisfy him. Faith reveals to him that God is present in another way in the Christian soul. This presence has a two-fold aspect: on the one hand it inspires terror, for God is holy; on the other, it expresses the ineffable condescension and love of God. For Augustine this presence, being the spiritual fruit of grace, is entirely supernatural. He penetrates to the heart of living Christianity which reaches out beyond reason strengthened by fear, as we find it in the Old Testament. This presence is known by faith, but it is perfected only by hope and charity and only in so far as the soul is truly pervaded by them. The Christian must be borne along by them in all his actions, outward or spiritual. This is the true perfection of man, a sublime wisdom, purely supernatural, both contemplative and active when it reaches the fullness of its growth.

For St Augustine, this perfection is mainly the work of the gifts of the Holy Spirit. These gifts imply a higher outpouring of grace in the soul, increasing as the soul frees itself from the senses and becomes more spiritual. The gifts of fear and piety represent the initial stages of this sublime action of God in the soul of every generous Christian obedient to the promptings of grace. Strength and counsel sustain him in his relations with his neighbour, while knowledge and understanding give him with regard to the created world and even God himself an enlightenment, relative but profound, which prepares the way for wisdom. Wisdom is the great mystical gift, a true union with God, bringing such a depth of peace and unity as can be achieved in this world, proportionate to the goodness of God as well as to the response of the creature.

The part played by wisdom, that gift of the Holy Spirit, is fully described by St Augustine in his work on the Trinity (Bk. 14). It is closely bound up with the sublime piety by which the Christian soul becomes a living image of the God in Three Persons, Father, Son and Holy Spirit. This image has its being only at the topmost point of the Christian soul, when, having learnt by faith that it is a child of God, the soul comes to "realize" this truth spiritually, with a disinterested love which takes complete possession of it and completes the union with

God. The image in question, which is an object of study for the theologian, is used by the praying soul, not to know, but to possess this God who deigns to give himself to be enjoyed by those who love him. Where the theologian analyses and distinguishes in order to observe the reality, the saint confines himself to loving contemplation of this God transcendent and yet present, One and yet Three in one Person: Father, Son and Holy Spirit. This contemplation is a sublime fruit of the theological virtues and the gifts of the Holy Spirit. It is the culminating point of Augustine's mysticism. Here Christ is still the way, by reason of his humanity, but he leads the praying and humble soul into the fullness of truth and life by union with the Three Persons.

St Augustine's mysticism, a pure echo of St Paul and St John, does not neglect the holiness of God as proclaimed by the ancient Law, of which the spiritual principles remain unchanged. It even clarifies the Law's demands, while increasing the spiritual forces which enable the Christian to respond to them within the framework of the theological virtues, for this is the atmosphere in which these sublime energies operate. They enable generous souls to rise by faith above the cares of this world, to live in heaven, as it were, by firm hope and fervent charity.

OTHER ANCIENT MYSTICS

Besides these true masters of prayer of the Great Century, there are other names which may be mentioned under various headings, according to the nature of their inspiration. The Christian poets, religious though they may be, cannot be identified with the mystics, even in the case of Ephrem the Syrian, a man of prodigious virtuosity and a saint, as was also Paulinus of Nola. Prudentius, though he has not the Church's guarantee, was none the less a Christian and of a lofty character. His work was not strictly mystical.

On the other hand, the works of two authors who are not venerated as saints may be put forward as a safe and valid source of mysticism. The older of the two, Diadochus, Bishop of Photike in Epirus at the time of St Leo, has left us an original treatise "on perfection". In it he lays emphasis, more than the other ancient masters of spirituality, on an inner sense, a spiritual inclination which detaches the soul from earthly pleasures and directs it towards an experience of God based on wisdom. This wisdom is closely bound up with a "theology", less a study than a sort of "contemplation", a mysterious union with God which is the fruit of grace and charity. At the same period, in the west, Julian Pomerus, a monk and priest of Arles (fifth century), a learned man, a philosopher and ascetic, is known only by his sole surviving written work, *The Contemplative Life*, more a pastoral treatise than one on mysticism. But the latter is not excluded. For the author, the spiritual life consists of two stages, an active stage characterized by the effort to achieve perfection, and a contemplative stage in which the soul has some experience of the eternal realities and finds strength for the spiritual apostolate with which Pomerus seems to have been chiefly concerned.

In the east, at the end of the same century, appeared the writings of a pure mystic of considerable stature who called himself "Dionysius the Areopagite".

We can allow him to keep this name, although in reality he is only a pseudo-Dionysius. He felt his teaching to be in accordance with tradition, and it is so in substance, though the form is new. The author wrote between 480 and 520. This mysterious person was probably a Palestinian bishop of Maiouma in the region of Gaza, Peter the Iberian, so called after his native country, Iberia or Georgia. His use of the name of St Paul's convert[1] was probably aimed at accrediting, if not a new doctrine, at least a fresh presentation of current Christian truths.

The work of the "Areopagite" does in fact make abundant use of the neo-Platonic philosophy of Proclus, so popular in the Gaza school at the end of the fifth century. It includes a short *Mystical Theology* (in five chapters) and three great works of general theology: *The Divine Names*, *The Celestial Hierarchy* and *The Ecclesiastical Hierarchy*. The recourse to

---

[1]Dionysius, Bishop of Athens, according to the early Fathers; the tradition which makes him out to be the first bishop of Paris is more recent and confuses him with the Dionysius sent to Gaul by Pope St Fabian, in the third century.

Platonism does not vitiate these theses which, on the whole, have a sound basis in revelation.

The mystical note rings out clearly in the work of "Dionysius", who exercised great influence in the Middle Ages. The doctrinal aspect predominates, even in the pages devoted to the exalted religious experience of contemplation. The latter is sometimes regarded under a negative aspect (silence, darkness), sometimes under a positive aspect (the knowledge of God, of sublime origin and thus truly divine): the mystic receives more than can be acquired by study (*non solum discens sed et patiens divina*). The hierarchies established by the author are based on this contemplation. It produces "a constant love of God and of divine things; the vision and knowledge of sacred truth; a divine sharing in the simple perfection of him who is supremely simple, the joy of contemplation which sustains the spirit and makes those who attain to it sharers in the nature of God" (*Ecclesiastical Hierarchy*, 1. 3). The "theology" which "Dionysius" has most in mind is a lofty and simple grasp of God, independent of any active exercise of the mind, but received from God as a sublime supernatural sharing in the divine life. It is, in fact, a sublime theological life, more heavenly than earthly.

The "Theology" of "Dionysius the Areopagite" was introduced into Latin and Byzantine spiritual circles by St Gregory the Great (†604) and St Maximus the Confessor (†662). The powerful personality of these great disciples toned down what was over philosophical in the work of Dionysius. They temper the theoretical bias by a wise insistence on the practical conditions required for the perfect Christian life.

St Gregory the Great, in his homilies, and particularly in the *Moralia,* has left us profound intuitions on the subject of contemplation, a lofty supernatural wisdom capable of giving a certain direct knowledge of God under many different forms. Sometimes he compares it to a distant vision seen in the darkness, as it were, sometimes to a spoken word, or rather a whisper. It is swift and often lasts but an instant, a simple prelude (*initia*) to the beatific vision. Its effects are powerful: profound humility, true contrition, heavenly peace and joy, a noble fervour in the search for God.

St Maximus the Confessor (580–662) lays emphasis on two points which do not stand out clearly in the work of Dionysius: namely, Christ and the virtue of charity. For him, Christ holds a central place, especially in the Christian life. Christ is not only the author of grace, he is its great model: the imitation of Christ is the great rule of the Christian life, in the struggle against evil, in prayer and contemplation, in the practice of virtue and especially of charity. Charity is the rule of the life of perfection. It necessarily includes the love of our neighbour, but it is essentially the love of God, and this is the source of its strength and of the privileges its brings with it. Charity it is which makes souls truly like God, endowing them with the sentiments in accord with their adoptive sonship, uniting them morally to God in that intimacy implied in the title of "spouse". It is through Christ that we receive all these gifts. He truly lives in souls by faith, and with him all the treasures of wisdom and knowledge are hidden there. If so many Christians fail to find them, only their own negligence is to blame.

CHAPTER VII

THE CHRISTIAN ASCETICS

PIONEERS OF THE FOURTH CENTURY

The asceticism with which we are concerned here is a way of perfection, organized doctrinally and socially. Its true exponents in the ancient world are not to be found until the fourth century. From the beginning, of course, the Church provided rules of perfection for all, and these were derived directly from the evangelical precepts. There were also fervent Christians, of either sex, who devoted themselves entirely to the pursuit of this ideal, but most of them lived apart in their own Christian or family circles, without forming any special group for this purpose. The virgins were an élite within the primitive "parish" communities rather than a separate group. It is only in the fourth century that we find that organized asceticism which was to exert so great an influence on the Christian way of life, first in the east and later in the west.

St Antony is rightly considered a pioneer in this respect, and there is no reason to dispute his title. St Paul the hermit, as described by St Jerome, is partly an edifying creation of the narrator. Very different, however, is the account by St Athanasius, our main source of knowledge of the great Egyptian monk who died in 356 at the age of 100. In 360 St Antony's life was written by his friend the Patriarch of Alexandria, and this book was both a revelation and a sermon for the whole Church. But, since the beginning of the century, the whole of eastern Christendom had been familiar with Egyptian monasticism. In the year 275, when he was about twenty-five, Antony had accepted literally Christ's call to total renunciation. He devoted himself to a life of prayer and solitude, first of all near his native village in central Egypt, not far from the river Nile, later in the desert, in the direction of the Red Sea. He was soon joined by hundreds of disciples, becoming their master and guide in the way of evangelical perfection.

His fundamental idea is the scorn of created things, which are as nothing in the eyes of God. The principle inspiring the movement is the contrast between the finite and the infinite. It would be a mistake, however, to reduce this to a philosophical concept. The word of Christ and his example, seen in the light of the Holy Spirit, formed the guiding force of these souls. The gift of knowledge, as the masters were later to point out, has the special purpose of making us understand the vanity of created things, while understanding penetrates the depths of our Saviour's message.

The specific doctrine of the solitaries is a twofold asceticism. The struggle against the Devil is prominent from the beginning, and this feature is particularly illustrated by the life of St Antony himself and by the treatise in which St Athanasius sums up his teaching. It is full of moral vigour which shines out in his unshakeable faith in Christ and his redemptive power, here manifested in the triumph over the Devil, and also in his expectation of the future life which gives an eschatological character to his thought, if not in the sense of an imminent return of Christ (a note which is perhaps exaggerated) at least in the sense of the greater value attached to the future life. It stands out again in his confidence in victory over the infernal powers and in his wise laws on the discerning of spirits.

In Africa itself, St Antony had imitators of a high order. At Nitria in Lower Egypt, about the year 325, thousands of monks grouped themselves round St Ammonius; and at Scetis on the borders of the Libyan desert, St Macarius the Great attracted similar numbers by his reputation for austerity. A spirit of pious emulation, sometimes a little noisy, reigned between the two groups, which remained faithful to Antony's theory of the eremitical life.

In Upper Egypt, higher up the Nile towards Ethiopia, we find the first great cenobitic centres, founded about the year

320 by St Pachomius (†346) at Tabennisi on an island in the Nile. A more rigid organization was formed shortly afterwards at Atripe, not far from Tabennisi by the austere Schenute (†450), while some distance away centres of cenobite women continued under the same inspiration.

The monastic institution crossed the borders of Egypt in the middle of the fourth century and spread to the east, where it was established on sites with a less favourable climate. It was soon to prosper in Syria, in the region of Antioch, where St John Chrysostom and St Jerome later came to do their training in the sacred school of asceticism. At this time it was already established in Cappadocia and Pontus, thanks to the activities of St Basil.

As for the west, it was first inspired by the revelations of St Athanasius, providentially exiled in Trier; but the great developments were to come at a later date. In Gaul in the middle of the fourth century St Martin founded Ligugé, near Poitiers, then Marmoutier near Tours, from which numerous foundations derived. The movement soon spread to the south of Gaul under this impulse and that of St Honoratus and Cassia, while St Augustine gave it a brilliant *début* in Latin Africa. These foundations, preceding the arrival of the Barbarians in the west, were the work of Providence: they laid the basis of a primarily spiritual Christian culture, rendered all the more necessary by the fall of the Empire, thus remotely anticipating the great reconstruction that came to be urgently necessary.

THE MONKS, THE GREAT MASTERS OF THE SPIRITUAL LIFE

Monasticism contained the germ of so many spiritual treasures that it was bound to exert a widespread influence. In fact, the whole Church was to benefit by it, for solitary meditation enabled the greatest minds to penetrate to the very heart of Christian reality. If all the revealed truths were developed by them on occasion, those concerning the spiritual life attracted them most, and it is in this field that the finest products of their searching and their religious experience are to be found.

St Basil, the principal founder of monasticism in the centre of Asia Minor, Pontus and Cappadocia, has left us spiritual works of the highest value, and they are more than just a rule in the juridical sense. The "Great Rules" are similar to the "Lesser Rules" as regards their application, but their emphasis is on doctrine rather than on the practices peculiar to the religious life. Neither in the fourth century nor at any subsequent period in antiquity was there an Order of St Basil, as there was later an Order of St Benedict. The title of the saint's *Moralia* indicates more clearly than the word Rule what was the true province of his interest and influence. All Christians may profit by a study of these texts borrowed from Scripture and explained from the universal viewpoint of evangelical perfection. It is obvious, however, that the monks for whom they were really intended derived the greatest benefit from them.

Thanks to St Basil, Asia Minor became, from the doctrinal point of view, one of the centres of influence of eastern monasticism. From his own family came his elder sister St Macrina who had founded a convent of nuns in Pontus, on the Iris, and his younger brother St Gregory, the future Bishop of Nyssa, who later wrote a life of St Macrina, a particularly famous treatise on virginity and four *opuscula* on perfection in the world and in the monastery. In other circles, also in Asia Minor, we find monks who wrote and who are famous for their ascetic teaching. Evagrius (†399) was to reflect honour on the great Egyptian monastery of Nitria, where he stood for a prudent and restrained version of Origenism. St Nilus the Ascetic († *circa* 430), the pride of Sinaï, also came from Asia Minor and had been a disciple of St John Chrysostom, as was probably his contemporary, Mark the Hermit. Both were spiritual writers of great prolificacy and lasting influence.

None of these authors enjoyed prestige comparable to that of St John Chrysostom, a priest of Antioch and a great preacher, who had previously lived as a monk in the neighbouring mountains, training himself to a life of intense prayer which influenced all his work, for the depth of his eloquence is proportionate to the fervour of his life as a Christian. His first written works were devoted to the monastic life; he defended it against its detractors and sang its praises as a true philosophy and as a human state superior to that of kings. He urged his best friends to embrace it and he would have remained in it himself or returned to it had not the duty of obedience impelled him to accept the priesthood and later the episcopate. As an exile in Taurus, quite near Antioch, he continued to teach on these lines, and this was one motive for his dismissal by a touchy court set on his destruction. The greatest voice of eastern Christendom had been trained in the school of Libanius and Demosthenes, but still more in that of St Paul whom he read and pondered in the solitude of the Syrian mountains. At the time of Chrysostom's oratorical triumphs in Antioch, the man who was to be the mouthpiece of Christianity in the west was on his way back to God. A few years his junior, St Augustine had wandered for a time into Manichaeism. He was converted in 386, at the very moment when the eastern Father was setting out on his career as a preacher. In 391, he himself ascended the bishop's chair, and, for close on forty years, never ceased to speak to his people and indeed to the whole Church in the west, for his words were so rich in wisdom and so Catholic that they were to resound through the Latin world from century to century, right up to our own time. The depth of his teaching is due no doubt in part to his own genius, but also to that profound wellspring of his inspiration, monastic solitude. At the time of his conversion he put into practice his dream of the contemplative life which had long haunted him and whose plan matured during his long retreat at Cassiacum. This plan he put into execution at Tagasta and later on when he was a priest at Hippo. Finally, as bishop, together with all his priests, he led a communal life which was a remote anticipation of the finest subsequent forms of sacerdotal monasticism. His writings on this subject constitute a very small part of his immense literary work, but it bears witness to the fertility of the institution which owed much to him and thanks to which he was able to carry on this superhuman work for such a length of time. His Rule is the earliest surviving code of western cenobiticism. As a code it is more spiritual than organic, hence its widespread influence in very varied circles. It continues to serve as an effective link between communities of both sexes. That he himself was capable of adding the necessary details can be seen from his treatise on "the work of monks", which demands that some should have manual occupations and all some sort of useful work. It can be seen, too, from his sermons (355–6), which lay down the conditions of common life for the clergy of Hippo grouped in the monastery around their bishop. For him, prayer was the essence of the religious life. He recommended, for example, the spoken word and the pen, the prayer of praise (*confessio*), and his work under this title is its immortal model. Here then is a real code of the Augustinian religious life, based on prayer and contemplation but directed towards a lofty and pure apostolate.

St Jerome was less influenced by monasticism, but he did take some part in it in the east, quite near Antioch, at the time when St John Chrysostom was undergoing his own ascetic training there. He did not live there for long, but he always remained a fervent upholder of asceticism and propagated it, first among the matrons and virgins of Rome and later in Bethlehem. His letters on asceticism are famous, and had a decisive influence on certain circles. His activity provided a link between east and west.

At the same period, but working along different lines, Cassian (†435), a former pupil of St John Chrysostom, came to establish monasticism in Marseilles. In his famous "Conferences" (*Collationes Patrum*), a collection of discussions with the best-known spiritual masters of Egypt at the end of the fourth century, he revealed to the Latin world the secret of the Egyptian solitaries. As a whole it is an excellent work, though certain pages of the thirteenth conference, where the necessity of grace in order to return to God is not made sufficiently clear, need toning down.

We may mention here another eastern ascetic work, of a somewhat later date, for it is a magnificent summary of the monastic spirituality of this period. It is the "Ladder to Heaven" of St John Climacus, a Syrian-born monk of the sixth or seventh century, who was probably Bishop of Sinaï. His work is a real spiritual code, perfectly adapted to the practice of the three theological virtues, and above all of charity. [The thirty chapters of this work make no claim to describe as many stages of sanctity in the sense of steps in the spiritual life as is sometimes imagined.] The work is a fine synthesis of the spiritual directives given to young recruits to the solitary life by the best and soundest masters.

ORGANIZERS OF THE MONASTIC LIFE
SINCE THE SIXTH CENTURY

It is clear from what has gone before that organized monasticism existed before the sixth century. However, a special effort was made from this period onwards, particularly in the west, and it is this aspect which we shall now consider. Passing over the doctrinal questions, such as Origenism in the east and Semi-Pelagianism in the west, which occasionally disturbed the monasteries, we shall confine our attention to the actual forms of the religious life, for in this field there is a certain development and, indeed, real progress.

St Caesarius of Arles, though not himself a monk, had a considerable influence on the monasteries, owing to his position as primate in the vast region occupied first by the Visigoths and afterwards by the Ostrogoths in South Gaul, until the Frankish conquest of Childebert who, in 536, changed the situation without prejudice to the advantages acquired by the Church. He introduced legislation for monks, and nuns, drawing inspiration from the so-called Augustinian Rule. He adapted one for monks, another for nuns, with some slight alterations which respected the primitive groundwork and general inspiration, within a framework of marked asceticism. Fasts and long offices were multiplied without regard for the ordinary customs of the monastic liturgy.

This note of austerity is still more marked in those foundations deriving from Irish monasticism. Christianity arrived late in the island of the Scots, later to become the Island of Saints, after its evangelization by the "Breton" St Patrick (†461). Historical criticism has questioned many aspects of his life, but the substance of it remains, particularly the fact of his apostolate as bishop from 432 onwards, and the organization of the beginnings of a hierarchy, with Armagh as the episcopal see and numerous monasteries as auxiliary centres. Neophytes crowded into the monasteries which were soon flourishing and full of apostolic zeal; so much so that the country, scarcely won to the faith, became itself an apostolic centre, sending numerous missionaries to the continent which had just been responsible for its conversion, for St Germanus of Auxerre had started the movement by consecrating St Patrick for this mission.

After Armagh, the principal centre of this Christian Odyssey was Bangor, on the north-east coast, facing towards Scotland, where thousands of monks assembled without detriment to other flourishing religious centres. Irish faith blossomed there with the spontaneous fervour characteristic of that country. That confidence in the value of human nature which the Breton monk Pelagius had championed in Italy and throughout the Empire at the beginning of the fourth century, was to take root and find powerful support in Britain itself, the only one existing at that time, before the emigration to Armorica took place. It is probable that this spirit also spread to the neighbouring island, then in the process of evangelization, and strengthened the tendency towards asceticism which was to become one of its characteristic features, yet without leading it into the excesses condemned by the Church. It is true that the Irish monks always showed exemplary generosity in their submission to the practice of the roughest austerities. In this respect they were courageous to the point of imprudence and practised heroism as if by instinct, if we are to believe the best established traditions. Moreover, the rule helped to sustain this fervour and violations of it were very severely punished. As in the east, the day was filled with prayer and work. But to this was added a new and very characteristic feature, namely the missionary spirit.

This "journeying for God" was a very different thing from the tours of information and edification often undertaken by eastern monks who wandered from desert to desert in search of teaching and good examples. If these were not without their abuses, they were often crowned with success, witness Cassian's "Spiritual Conferences" which are masterpieces of their kind. It was a doctrinal and spiritual apostolate that these "visitors" had in mind. The travelling monks of Ireland were true missionaries in the modern sense of the word, without detriment to their life as monks. Their work was carried out by forming religious groups for the purpose of bringing pagans to the faith and Christians to a more perfect life. The whole of western Europe, particularly on both sides of the Rhine and on the flanks of the Jura and the Alps, reaped great benefit from this wave of apostolic activity.

St Columbanus remains the type of the Irish missionary monk. Carried away by the spirit of zeal at the age of fifty, he founded, near Luxeuil in Gaul, a real monastic colony of which he was the head and which he armed with a staunch apostolic spirit. Driven out after thirty years, he set out again towards the east, founding more monasteries in Germany, Switzerland and Italy, where he started his last monastery at Bobbio on the Po in 614, a year before his death. He remains famous, not only for his tireless zeal, but also for his austerity which later was happily tempered by the Benedictine spirit, without losing all its primitive originality due to the character of his race and still more to his fervent faith.

The most important work in the organization of ancient monasticism was done by St Benedict († between 543 and 553). The abbot of Monte Cassino drew his inspiration from the most famous rules of east and west, those of St Pachomius, St Basil, St Augustine, Cassian and also from the lives of the Fathers. The characteristics of his work are the part played by a fixed hierarchy, stability of life and the moderation of the practices imposed in prayer and work, a relative moderation, for his demands are great and require a real effort. This effort is sustained by a moderate spirituality, accessible to all and proportionate to the character and learning of the various monks of the community. The introduction of the priesthood under the influence of St Gregory the Great contributed much to the development of spirituality suited to the needs of individual souls without prejudice to the framework established by the founder. This combination of hierarchical and doctrinal features made the Rule of St Benedict a major force in the Church, at a time when spiritual élites could scarcely be formed and maintained outside the monasteries.

St Gregory also gave a powerful impetus to liturgical organization, and in this respect he also strengthened the monastic life, particularly of the Benedictine Order, of which this has always been a salient feature. Psalmody and chant were broadly fixed according to the principles laid down and established in St Gregory's time and under his inspiration. The liturgical life of the Church has been based on them for centuries and today she still looks to them for her main directives in this field.

Constantinople, the brilliant capital of the eastern Empire, also became a monastic centre, such was the number of monasteries, particularly for men, founded in the city itself or in the neighbourhood, on both sides of the Bosphorus. The link between them was little more than a spiritual one, mainly based on the so-called "Rules" of St Basil which are all, the Greater as well as the Smaller, doctrinal directives of a mainly practical nature, intended to assist the religious in their spiritual life.

We must, however, refer to one original creation which anticipates many subsequent western institutions in the Middle Ages: namely the Acemetes, which means literally "non-sleepers". It was really a sort of perpetual adoration based on an organization of the liturgical offices in such a way as to ensure their uninterrupted chanting. The initiator in this field was St Alexander the Syrian, who had founded a monastery of this type in his own land, near the river Euphrates. He tried in vain to found another at Antioch, and later in the city of Constantinople, about the year 430; but he was entirely successful on the coast of Asia, not far from the Bosphorus. He assembled up to four hundred monks, speaking various languages, and these he divided into groups which took turns in the choir to ensure the *laus perennis*. For a long time other monastic houses, even from the city, looked to them for a method of prayer and even for monks to organize it in their own communities. Interesting as this institution was, it constituted only a subsidiary form of Byzantine monasticism.

The Acemetic institution suffered considerably from the interminable war waged by the Iconoclasts who, for more than a century, wrought havoc on the most fervent of the Byzantine monasteries. However, there was a fine recovery with the Studites, who, at the end of the eighth century, managed to reorganize it in the capital city itself, at the *Studion*. St Theodore assembled hundreds of monks there who carried on the best of the ancient traditions, adding to them the hieratic style of iconography so dear to Byzantine piety. The Council of Nicaea had recognized its legitimacy, and it has persisted to our day, to the great benefit of monastic, and indeed of all Christian piety. It remains one of the characteristic features of religious life in the east and particularly in Byzantium.

CHAPTER VIII

SPIRITUAL TRENDS

The foregoing analyses, however summary in some cases, will at least have demonstrated the great spiritual vitality of the ancient Church. The many branches and the abundant fruit they produced bear witness to the vigour of its life and to the fact of its divine origin, since sacred history expressly declares it and its works confirm what history reveals. It remains for us to make a general survey of this mass of spiritual phenomena, rapidly discussed in these pages, in order to bring out the points of contact between them. These are to be found in the deeper trends underlying the various spiritual groups which we have constantly encountered. Confining ourselves to what is most characteristic, we shall relate these trends with the great doctrinal schools of the ancient Church, tracing their adaptation to the new conditions imposed on Christianity from the middle of the first century, a relative development, but nevertheless a real and profitable one.

THE SCHOOL OF ALEXANDRIA

Alexandria was clearly a providential meeting-point between the spirit of Christianity, based on faith, and the Greek spirit based on reason. Origenism, the most outstanding fruit of this encounter, remained fundamentally Christian at heart, in spite of the audacity of certain innovators which was tempered by the best bishops of Alexandria in the third century and particularly in the fourth and fifth; it will be sufficient to quote the illustrious names of St Athanasius and St Cyril. Not all the Alexandrine Doctors were Origenists, far from it, but all the

Catholic thinkers of this school shared a characteristic preoccupation with God. The things of God were truly the starting-
point of all their speculations and the direct aim of all their
ascetic effort, when they gave themselves up to asceticism like
St Antony or sought to propagate it, as St Athanasius did so
successfully. These monks, with their long fasts and constant
struggles with the Devil, were also eager for silence and prayer,
to which they devoted long hours of the day and night. St
Athanasius, who wrote so admiringly of them, deserves to be
taken at his word.

A famous representative of the Origenist type of Alexandrine
piety was Evagrius Ponticus (†399), a monk of Nitria where
Origen was long held in honour. He himself came from Pontus,
was a man of great learning and had known St Gregory in
Constantinople. He enjoyed great prestige. St Maximus the
Confessor borrowed the best of his thought: the three steps
in the spiritual ascent; the doctrine of *apatheia* in the practice
of the virtues and the part played by love in the preparation
for contemplation; the theory of pure prayer from which all
imaginative activity is excluded. In his vast and complex work
he was led to employ theories of a dangerous character which
compromised him gravely and caused him to be condemned
two centuries later as an Origenist.

St Cyril of Alexandria (†444) was to become the great
spiritual authority in Egypt in the fifth century. More than any
other person of that period he emphasized the part played by
the Holy Spirit as a source of sanctification in every Christian.
It is true that we are sanctified by the whole Trinity, but this
work is carried out by the Spirit "who is its perfume, its quality
and its fortifying power", the "spring of living water welling
up to eternal life", the "seal imprinted (on the soul) to restore
its resemblance to God". It is even on this action of the Holy
Spirit that Cyril, like all the Fathers of the fourth century, bases
his proof of the divinity of the Spirit. The Holy Spirit deifies,
therefore he is God; fire is only to be kindled from fire; only
God can make us sharers in the Divine Nature. The Holy
Spirit, who is God, is united to the soul that he sanctifies by a
simple moral union, relative yet real, very close and fertile, as
he had been united to the first man, and it is thus that man is

"deified". The formulas here quoted, and the images employed to express a lofty reality, are a fine illustration of the realistic character of Alexandrine piety. Far from denying sanctifying grace, as has been wrongly believed, Cyril attributes it to the Holy Spirit; this appropriation explains everything, provided that it is viewed in the light of the Greek conception of the Trinity: we can then seek the analogies existing between justification and the personal attributes of the Holy Spirit, and these analogies are the true basis of appropriation. This realism of faith, thus leading to mysticism, is the salient feature of the Alexandrine tradition, always careful to lay its emphasis on God and the divine action on souls.

THE SCHOOL OF ANTIOCH

The School of Antioch, especially from the fourth century onwards, practised a sort of higher Christian morality, divine also in many respects but closer to human reality. Its finest exponent was St John Chrysostom. The accusation of Origenism made against him was most unjust; St Epiphanius, deceived at first by the treacherous calumnies of Theophilus of Alexandria, recognized his own mistakes, and Theophilus himself did not mention any of these grievances at the Council of the Oak (called thus from its meeting place, a suburb of Chalcedon). In point of fact, Chrysostom has much more in common with the anti-Origenist school of Antioch. Moreover, a strong sense of tradition enabled him to avoid the dangers latent in the tendencies of that school to which he owed his scientific religious education.

Above all, in the field of Christology, he was careful to maintain the personal unity of our Saviour, avoiding the over-precise dualist formulas of his master Diodorus. He affirms that Christ is one, while comparing his humanity to a temple in which he lives. He makes no attempt to fathom the mystery. In what way is Christ one? "Don't worry about that," he says. "Christ himself knows it."

He took the same line in the matter of the Trinity. One of his main accusations against the Antinomians is that they want to "understand" God. He had the sense of mystery and this humility together with his obedience to tradition preserved him from stumbling. The Pelagians claimed that he denied original sin; St Augustine refuted them, and with justice. Although his work contains no theory of original sin as precise as that of the Bishop of Hippo, the doctrine of the fall of humanity is clearly stated in it.

St Ephrem the Syrian, founder of a famous school at Edessa, whither he retired when the Persians invaded Nisibis after 360, also belongs to the school of Antioch, even as regards his mysticism. By the best of his spiritual tendencies he prepared the way for St John Chrysostom. It was in the monasteries, and in the field of ethics and asceticism, that he exercised most influence. His piety had the surest basis of faith, aided by a true devotion to the Blessed Virgin Mary.

The basis of his teaching is a very clear affirmation of our freedom of will. Man was made in the image of God as regards his freedom and his dominion over all creation, his capacity for receiving the gifts of God and the ability of his mind to conceive and apply itself to everything. In the case of our first parents, this natural image of God was accompanied by precious supernatural gifts, including a certain outward radiation of light, which veiled their nakedness from their own eyes and was nothing but a reflection of the sublime gifts in their souls. All this was lost by sin, but the freedom of the will remains, weakened and infirm as it is. St Ephrem is very insistent on this point. Fallen man needs grace but grace assists him without doing violence to his freedom.

St Ephrem prefers to regard the Christian life as a spiritual combat. He provides arms against all the vices, and especially the eight capital ones; particularly he recommends fasting, temperance, prayer, the reading of Scripture. The virtues he seems to prefer are charity, virginity, patience, humility and penitence, the last of which he often discusses. He discourses forcefully on the vanity of earthly things and urges fervent souls to withdraw from the world. He wrote many instructions for monks; we need mention only his short treatise on "the Spiritual Life", another on the training of monks and two *opuscula* "on Virtue", and "to a Novice". Finally, as a simple deacon, he wrote a small treatise praising the dignity of the priesthood and the holiness of life that it demands.

The work of Diadochus, Bishop of Photike in Epirus, entitled "A Hundred Chapters on Spiritual Perfection", seems to
belong more to the ascetic trends of Antioch than to Alexandrine theology. The author lived in the fifth century and is
scarcely known except for his spiritual activity, particularly
against the Euchites, false mystics of Asia Minor (condemned
at Ephesus in 431), who explained temptations by the joint
indwelling in man of God and the Devil. His wise writings
contain excellent advice for the struggle against the passions
and the Devil; he recommends the principal moral virtues,
continence, temperance, poverty, obedience and humility, but
with a marked emphasis on the spiritual life: prayer, recollection, silence, peace of mind. Nevertheless the basis of Diadochus' teaching is mainly mystical and this we must describe in
its broad outlines.

Chapters I–II set out the basic principles, the theological
virtues inspiring a spiritual desire for God, which is true wisdom; it finds expression in apostolic exhortations, when its
"very plenitude does not render words impossible". The main
theme of his teaching is this "spiritual desire" for God which
fills the soul with sweetness, the fruit of the Divine Presence.
The "desire for God" is a spiritual sense by which the Holy
Spirit moulds souls in the image of the Creator. By successive
touches, the Divine Artist completes his work in souls. According to Diadochus, this gradual formation takes place in three
stages: a period of sweetness, at the beginning of the spiritual
life; then, a long period of struggle against the assaults of the
Devil and the senses, during which the soul is purified and
gradually acquires perfect possession of the spiritual sense;
when this sense is granted, the soul is totally transformed by it.
Such a soul is often filled with a sublime infused activity of
charity which "surpasses faith" (*supra fidem consistere*), for
"he who is drawn to God by ardent love is then much greater
than his faith; he is given over entirely to his desire". This
desire, which has its source in charity enriched by the spiritual
sense, confirms him in a state above that of mere faith, which
in itself is imperfect.

THE WESTERN SCHOOL

At the same period, early in the fifth century, Latin Africa witnessed the fruition of a doctrinal work which, under Providence, was to provide a synthesis of the finest spiritual elements contained in the ancient schools and transmit them to the west before its invasion by the barbarians. From his great centres of activity, Carthage and Hippo, St Augustine's influence spread to Europe and the east, after he himself had benefited from the fresh contributions of that extensive spiritual learning which answered the needs of his genius, so totally applied to the great problems of life and thought. In his philosophy alone, we might detect an affinity with the school of Alexandria, though he has no share in its excesses. At the age of nineteen, he had been conquered by the genius of Plato. But it was at the age of thirty that he first really knew him, through the recently translated writings of Plotinus. These filled him with enthusiasm in spite of increasingly clear reservations due to his faith, reborn under the influence of St Ambrose at Milan, as we see from the *Confessions*. Through his reading of Plotinus he became, instinctively, more and more attached to Plato himself, until he was entirely dominated by his thought, as was the case when he wrote *The City of God*. In fact, it was in a God of pure Spirit that he was to find the true source of all ideas, an absolutely transcendent source which nevertheless acts on that masterpiece, the human spirit, essentially united to the body, but superior to it, since it is called to a life of immortality and, in spite of its shortcomings, has an exalted destiny.

Yet, for Augustine, this high philosophy of the spirit is only a handmaid, less significant in herself than because of her activity in the service of that living theology, which, far more than his philosophy, marks his affinity with the great Doctors of Alexandria, providentially introduced to him by St Ambrose of Milan, to whom they formed an inexhaustible source of inspiration in his Christian life and preaching.

At the same time, Augustine was laying the sure doctrinal foundations of a living Christian ethic. The keynote of this synthesis is awareness of God. Its spirit is derived from the *Confessions*. The work as a whole testifies to a living presence of God in the author. This is best described in Books 9 and 10, and its decisive features are fixed in Book 13, in accordance with a method only artificially based on Scripture: in point of fact, what he describes is a lofty mystical experience which finds its expression in action as well as prayer. Books 11 and 12 are an attempt to apply to the first chapters of Genesis a superior method of doctrinal research suited to the great problems, particularly that of time. For the author, this is one of the problems in which the difference between Creator and creature is most clearly illustrated; the Creator, living outside of time, in eternity, in his centre of activity which is equally a centre of repose; the creature, always imprisoned within it in spite of his attempts to escape. These and other similar problems were taken up again in the twelve books on *The Letter of Genesis,* a veritable summa of penetrating questions and answers on the loftiest aspects of the natural and supernatural knowledge of the period. Though the work may be a scientific one, we must not forget the spiritual atmosphere and the time in which it was written.

During these same years, St Augustine was working hard on his great masterpiece on the Trinity, a profound investigation of the nature of God himself, with special reference to the Divine Persons. Of course, he drew his material from Scripture, but he made use of reason to classify this material and enrich it by a series of analyses and syntheses which anticipate the work of the medieval universities. His pages on the relation which is the basis of personality in God are a work of genius. But still more important and more original are the last eight books of this work (8–15), in which the author examines the human soul with extraordinary acuteness and subtlety, to discover in it the closest possible resemblance to the life of the Trinity.

Thus the soaring flights of the Alexandrine school and the disciplined scriptural research of the school of Antioch find a living synthesis in the work of St Augustine. In it they also find their completion, for the last twenty years of his life were devoted to examining another aspect of Christianity, namely that which is described in *The City of God,* a theological rather than a historical work, however great the part history plays in it. In face of the imminent ruin of society which he foresaw, Augustine's thought reached out to the one unchanging city, the heavenly life in which the elect would form a true and imperishable society, the times preceding it having no meaning or lasting value for men, except in so far as they can make use of them to direct their lives towards that end.

Such are the broad outlines of the doctrinal synthesis which was the dying Augustine's legacy to the west, of which he was the great master in the doctrinal field. It is by no means certain that their true tendencies have been faithfully observed and maintained. The Pelagian controversies forced the saint into taking up rigid positions of resistance which could and should be softened by an overall view of his work, particularly his insistence on the importance of supernatural wisdom based on a true life of the spirit, without prejudice to the essential unity of man or the universality of the call to salvation. Any restrictions in these respects were the result of various limitations of the vast spiritual plan drawn up by Augustine on a level to which men too rarely rise, so that they tend to distort it.

Among those who expounded Augustine's spiritual teaching with the greatest authority and breadth, we must mention St Gregory the Great who, long before he became pope, was guided and inspired by his writings and who for fourteen years (590–604) took advantage of the authority of his office to apply his principles in every sphere of Christian life. Before him, Pomerus, a monk and priest of Arles, had set out these principles in a volume devoted to the pastoral life, under the devout title of *The Contemplative Life.* St Gregory returned to this theme, applying it particularly to the monks to whom his *Moralia* was addressed, and through them the whole Church profited by it. In reality, this work is neither strictly moral nor pastoral, but rather spiritual in the modern sense of the word. His spirituality is mystical in tendency, for his thought rises to these heights, and in this respect he is truly in line with St Augustine. Many more examples might be quoted. There is nothing in them to weaken the principal theses of St Augustine's work, nor do they seem to add anything essential from the point of view of our general survey. St Augustine laid down spiritual principles: they constitute a synthesis of the spiritual values already recognized, at least in substance, from early Christian times, especially in the east, and it is these which were most fully appreciated and applied in western Christian life.

St Gregory's influence was effective in imprinting these achievements on western Christendom; this was due to the pre-eminent position held by the papacy, the inheritor of the power of the keys entrusted to St Peter and the hierarchic centre without which the whole Church could have no true unity. This authority made itself most strongly felt through the monastic institutions so indispensable to the western Church in those troubled times, which lasted for several centuries. This doctrinal and practical support was to be highly beneficial, though its full effects were only revealed at a later date.

THE BYZANTINE SCHOOL

In the east, too, at this period, the Church was undergoing great trials in many countries, even though the centre established by Constantine remained inviolate, and gathered round itself, at least in name, the ancient patriarchates of the fourth century. From the fourth century onwards, increasingly, Constantinople became Byzantium once again, in spite of a certain greatness in both religious and political spheres. It is with the former aspect that we are here concerned. The secessions from the Church caused by the heresies, which were a real scourge to the nation (Nestorianism, especially in Syria; Monophysism, mainly in Egypt), were aggravated by the inroads made by the Persians and Arabs in the south, and the Slavs in the north and, in spite of magnificent recoveries in south and west, Byzantium became a proud but lonely bastion of the faith. This stronghold was at least a Christian and even a mystical one, if by this we imply the official intervention of religion in all the mechanism of the State and in all branches of society. For the spiritual foundations, we must look more closely.

There is to be noticed above all, in this Byzantine Church, the existence of what might be called the "Byzantine school", a

title which justifies the maintenance of at least a nominal
doctrinal influence over the so-called "Orthodox" Christians.
This word designates those eastern Churches moulded by Constantinople and remaining faithful to her spirit. But her terri-
tory, from the sixth century onwards, had become very
restricted, for in spite of Justinian's prestige and his ephemeral
triumphs in the west, the south-eastern section of the Empire
gradually crumbled away. Turning in on itself, the Empire
held its own and later made spiritual conquests among the
Slavs who received the Christian Faith from it. Hence the importance of this religious group and of its spirit.

The Byzantine Church remained fully Catholic until the
ninth century and afterwards, in spite of the crises which tore
her apart. Falling back on her own resources and dominated
by the Court, she had no real thinkers comparable to those of
the ancient schools of the east. Of these she has preserved the
memory, in a conventionalized form, owing to the three hier-
archs to whom she appeals, St Basil and St Gregory Nazianzen,
those neo-Alexandrines of the fourth century, and St John
Chrysostom, the pride of Antioch, venerated as a martyr, for
his exile and tragic death did much to further his cause. In
actual fact, these names are glorious memories rather than
living forces of inspiration. Even the eloquence which played
so great a part in this Church was more formal than that of
those ancient masters. At least she was to have the merit of
transmitting to the Church the testimony of an ardent devotion
to our Lady, for it is in her homilies that the most formal evidence in favour of the Immaculate Conception and Assumption
of Mary have been found.

Among the masters who left their mark on Byzantine thought
and spirituality, we must not omit Dionysius the Areopagite, a
theologian probably from the borders of Syria and Egypt who
wrote at the end of the fifth century; his work was introduced
to Constantinople in the sixth century, under Justinian, and was
finally adopted there by St Maximus the Confessor in the
seventh century. To further the ends of a solid Christian faith,
this work made use of a very marked neo-Platonic philosophy,
though the application of it to theology was superficial, more
verbal than profound and quite different from the use of it

made by St Augustine in the west. Nevertheless, this mixture had its value and represents a genuine doctrinal affinity. As for his mysticism, it was theoretical rather than a powerfully experienced reality.

The true spiritual master of the Byzantine Church is St Maximus the Confessor, a profound theologian, who died a martyr in defence of the complete humanity of Christ, minimized by the Monothelites in the seventh century. His theology was accompanied by an ardent devotion to the Man-God, the imitation of whom he fervently recommended in the first pages of one of his ascetic works: and his mysticism, closely allied to charity, blossomed into contemplation. Thus he tempered the intellectualism of "Dionysius" while making use of his views on the "Hierarchies" in a "Mystagogia" inspired by that author. His conception of charity leads to a true mystical union, even without ecstasy, and in these respects Maximus is one of the greatest spiritual masters of antiquity, and the most reliable of that school of which he is the perfect representative. The exterior brilliance of this school in liturgy and art and the somewhat artificial eloquence of the best religious orators of the Byzantine Church, all due to the influence of the Imperial Court, were happily tempered by the depth of his spirituality.

St Maximus was a monk. He thus belonged to those chosen Christians who had first fled the cities in search of the peace of God and had afterwards invaded them in order to bring that peace to souls exposed to corruption. In face of the attractions of luxury and worldly splendour which the Byzantine Court embodied in the eyes of the common people, the monks led a life of recollection, penitence and prayer in the very centre of the city, right opposite the sumptuous palace of the Basileus. The iconoclastic Emperors of the seventh century were particularly offended by this contrast and tried to break this opposition by destroying monasticism, for the monasteries were the favourite asylums of the defenders of the icons. The Studites carried on this struggle with spectacular vigour and emerged victorious after a hundred years and as many battles. The bishops almost invariably yielded to the Imperial will; the monks resisted it, supported by the popes whose authority was recognized in theory by the Byzantine Church (even the

Novellae inserted by Justinian in his code testify to this), and they finally triumphed in the ninth century.

From a historical point of view, the feast of "Orthodoxy", established in 843, is a reminder of this religious epic in a truly Catholic sense, although later interpretations have given it a very different character. Genuine orthodoxy is based on the notes of the Church which the Creed of Constantinople in 381 summed up in four points and which the Byzantine liturgy itself repeats every Sunday: *Unam, sanctam catholicam et apostolicam Ecclesiam.* In the second century, an eastern Father, St Irenaeus, reminded the west that this catholicity and apostolicity of the Churches was, in fact, realized by union with the Church of Peter which is in Rome. The Byzantine Church of which we have been speaking knew this, especially in its spiritual élites, and therein lay its strength. Orthodoxy, far from being itself a criterion of truth, stands in need of one. And the Byzantine Church can find it, still speaking to her in her history and liturgy, if the dross left by the passions on a historically glorious and fundamentally Christian foundation is disregarded. The Byzantine school could, properly understood, draw from their tragic "isolation" all the Churches who appeal to its authority and often fall into spiritual lethargy through lack of the sustaining strength of Catholicity. What a vast field for its influence to spread!

CHAPTER IX

GREAT DEVOTIONS OF THE ANCIENT SPIRITUAL WRITERS

We have examined many aspects of the Fathers' writings, always from the point of view of the spiritual life. It is time now to classify the results of our investigations. We have not sought to determine dogmas or to demonstrate the origins of any particular theological synthesis of a speculative or ethical character. We have been concerned mainly with believers living their faith and finding in it a real fullness of human and Christian life.

This perfect life is achieved on a supernatural level, but nature is by no means excluded. The men whose activity we have considered are really men and not angels; they shared our weaknesses and our sufferings, overcoming them by the firmness of their faith and above all by the strength of their supernatural love. Most of them were saints and several set an example of outstanding virtue. So they were not merely theologians, technicians writing dissertations on the sources of faith and the exact significance of the words of revelation; beyond these formulas and the scholarly research they demand, they sought the divine realities expressed in them, uniting their whole being to those realities by charity. They were in fact spiritual writers rather than theorists. They were drawn to the divine life for its own sake and for the sake of the life it communicates, more than by the quest for knowledge of similar gifts, and that is what distinguishes the Fathers from theologians of every period.

For them, in a sense, all things revolved round Jesus Christ, the single object of their thoughts. As in the case of the Apostles, our Saviour was the centre of their preoccupations. In fact, they made their own that saying of St Paul when he declared to the Corinthians that he wished to know only Jesus Christ and him crucified (1 Cor. 2. 2). But in studying the Fathers, we quickly realize that Christ, far from acting as a limitation, is in fact a universal starting-point and that all things of living interest to man are related to him. We have analysed this fact in the various chapters of this book. We are now in a position to make a synthesis of it, starting from that central point where all things meet in God. However veiled the mystery of Christ is and must remain, it is nonetheless a source of wealth for those who approach it with piety, schooled by him, to study the many aspects of it unfolded in the thought and prayer of Christian antiquity. The cultus of the Three Persons, so dear to the Fathers, takes the Christian beyond the limits of devotions in the usual sense, but on it all of them are based.

THE THREE DIVINE PERSONS

In Christ, the mystery of the God in Three Persons is revealed, and this mystery was, from the beginning, the Fathers' main source of piety.

In the face of paganism, the Christians were bound to emphasize God's unity, but this did not prevent them from affirming the divinity of Christ, and shedding their blood in defence of it. But already at this period and in the earliest patristic writings, as in those of the Apostles themselves, the Three Persons are proclaimed as God, a God who is one and experienced as such in a spiritual life of great intensity, in which a higher power makes itself felt, a single complex power whose three-fold source, Father, Son and Holy Spirit, is named in the Gospels. In his very life, the Christian is brought into contact with their sublime reality. Before yielding to curiosity about this subject the first Christians lived this truth intensely in their souls, and the writings of a man like St Irenaeus show us how deeply they entered into the very life of God with their whole spiritual being, long before the great Trinitarian controversies began. For these Christians who lived their Christianity instead of writing copious dissertations on it, as the philosophers of other times were to do, the Three Persons are always in the foreground of their thought and prayer, the two being closely linked together. The life of piety provided these masters with a wealth of doctrine sufficient for all the needs of the soul in that time of combat and prayer.

The Fathers of the fourth century who brought about the triumph of the traditional faith in the divinity of the Word, the Son of God, equal to the Father, had recourse less to speculative theology than to the Christian life. Such in particular was the case of the greatest of them all, St Athanasius. His true source of inspiration was an ardent piety, content with simple formulas borrowed from Holy Scripture, because he had penetrated their depths of meaning by the intuitions of the heart and of grace. Hence the certitude which cannot be explained by human causes. The Cappadocian masters were also men of prayer, trained in solitude, who drew from their contemplation formulas capable of bringing back many hesitant minds to the true faith, in spite of the obvious gaps in their speculative theology. The life of prayer made up for the deficiency of their knowledge in this field.

The Doctor who achieved the most penetrating insight into this sublime mystery was certainly St Augustine. His teaching was not definitive, for there can be none such. The fact of the Three Persons in God was incontestably the most important in his life: it crowned and completed all the questing of his insatiable spirit. In it he found peace of mind and heart, because he lived this mystery so deeply in his prayer. Many pages of the first seven books of *The Trinity* are easily understood, but the whole of the second part of that work is based on his lofty insight into the analogies between the human soul and the divine Being, Pure Spirit and transcendent Life, one in nature, yet three Persons. Here the intuitions of the mind are based on those received in prayer directed to the highest possible object. We have shown how St Augustine found in the

Christian soul, ready to be taught by grace to the point of wisdom, a perfect image of God in Three Persons, yet one in nature. This image, perhaps no more than an image for the intellectual seeker, becomes the highest prayer of union in the Christian soul who lives by God present and dwelling within it.

JESUS CHRIST, THE INCARNATE WORD

It was the revelation of the Man-God which first made known, with decisive force, the fact of the Three Persons in God, and the clear recognition of them establishes the basis of the mystery of the Incarnation without being sufficient to express it. Here a new problem arises, and from the start it is closely bound up with a third, one of piety: namely, the divine motherhood of Mary. Indeed it was because of the title, Mother of God, given to the mother of Jesus in the east from the fourth century onwards, that the controversies arose and Mary's great privilege was at last solemnly proclaimed. In this case the intuitions of Christian piety were the basis of the conciliar definitions, and this fact must be clearly understood, not only from the dogmatic point of view but also, and perhaps above all, from that of the Christian life in which it holds a prominent place.

Mary would not be the Mother of God, if Jesus Christ was not God in person, and solely God as regards his personality. If, in Jesus Christ, there was a human person side by side with the divine person, Mary would be the mother of the former and not the mother of God; she would be a mother like any other earthly mother, and however great a thing human maternity may be, it has nothing divine about it. For to be truly the Mother of God, her son, as a person, must be God alone. Now, when we use the word person in connection with a human being, we mean he who acts, speaks, thinks and loves in that living and complex whole which we call human nature, body and soul. All this belongs to a being who makes use of it, but who in some sense transcends it; it does not possess, but is possessed by, a person; and, in the case of Jesus Christ, that person is God, the Son of God, infinite Wisdom, the Word who came into the world to help man to rise again towards God.

Faced with a mystery so simple and yet so complex, St Cyril of Alexandria must have possessed insight of a high order to grasp at once, in spite of the shortcomings of contemporary philosophy in this field, the danger of the formulas put forward by men of learning and subtlety like Nestorius and his supporters, whose good intentions were always beyond dispute. The popes, guardians of the faith, were informed by St Cyril and gave him unreserved support. In spite of all subsequent difficulties due to the direct but imperfect formulas which he used in his desire to penetrate straight to the heart of the mystery involved, the intervention of the Patriarch of Alexandria was decisive. It was the work of Providence, and the saint's other writings clearly show that he had been excellently prepared, by prayer and study, to carry out this supremely important mission. If, at this hour of decision, he was able to be the Doctor of the Incarnation and to present his message with such clarity, it was due to a spiritual preparation to which the whole of his doctrinal work bears witness.

But the mystery of the Man-God is not fully expressed by the affirmation of a single divine person; it remains to define the natures involved, for, in order to be God incarnate he must have both the divine nature common to the Three Persons and the human nature which is here added to it, without a personality of the same order, but benefiting by the sublime personality of the Word. This humanity is in no way mutilated, and this was the danger which had to be faced immediately after the rejection of dualism. In Alexandria and elsewhere, indeed, there was soon a tendency in many circles to insist, not only on the divine person, but also on the divine nature, at the expense of the human nature in Jesus Christ. The Church had already rejected those who, in their desire to safeguard the personality of Christ had refused the higher faculty of reason to his human nature. Once again she reacted vigorously, loudly proclaiming the absolute completeness of his humanity. Pope St Leo assumed personal control and by his efforts the definitive formula touching the essential elements of the Incarnation was found and approved.

Here again we must admire the divine intervention against Monophysism, which questioned the humanity of Christ and with it the very basis of Christianity. We cannot only regard St Leo's action as providential, so firmly did he uphold the ancient faith, putting an end to all attempts at merging the divine and human natures of our Saviour. The sects multiplied in vain. Not only were they condemned in principle, but the cultus of our Saviour's humanity was to profit by their errors, as it did two centuries later by the condemnation of Monothelism, due mainly to St Maximus the Confessor, who contrived to join to the cultus of the humanity of Christ a true spiritual and mystical doctrine the results of which can be seen in the teaching given by St Bernard in the Middle Ages and a special application of it in the modern devotion to the Sacred Heart.

CHRIST, REDEEMER AND PRIEST

The mystery of the Redemption is another aspect of the Incarnation. Yet it has not given rise to as much discussion, although its importance was recognized from the beginning: towards the end of the second century St Irenaeus wrote forcefully and copiously on the subject.

Is the Redemption not the very purpose of the Incarnation? The ancient writers, relying on St Paul, seem to have no doubt about it, and this aspect of the mystery is the very heart of Christianity. St Athanasius, the great defender of the divinity of Christ, the Word made flesh, recognizes that Redemption is the purpose of the Incarnation, though he is more concerned with the latter. In the eyes of this Patriarch of Alexandria the simple fact of the Word having become man is so important that the rest follows as an obvious corollary. Not that he underestimates the importance of the redemptive aspect; but he is too much concerned with the other to be drawn to it yet; the contemplation of the Word Incarnate is enough: it is everything for him.

None of the ancient Doctors laid such an emphasis on the Redemption as St Augustine. He does not regard it merely as having a moral value and the power of example, he also examines profoundly the exacting conditions of the satisfaction for sin, an offence of infinite magnitude, calling for proportionate reparation. In the *Confessions* he devoted moving lines to this subject which are quoted here, for they show with what an accent of piety the saint treated so lofty a subject:

But the true Mediator, whom in the secret of your mercy you have shown to men and sent to men, that by his example they might learn humility—the Mediator between God and men, the man Christ Jesus, appeared between sinful mortals and the immortal Just One: for like men he was mortal, like God he was Just; so that, the wages of justice being life and peace, he might, through the union of his own justice with God, make void the death of those sinners whom he justified by choosing to undergo death as they do. He was shown forth to holy men of old that they might be saved by faith in his Passion to come, as we by faith in his Passion now that he has suffered it. As man he is Mediator (1 Tim. 2. 5): but as Word, he is not something in between, for he is equal to God, God with God, and together one God (with the Father and the Holy Spirit).

How much thou hast loved us, O good Father, who hast not spared even thine own Son, but delivered him up for us wicked men! (Rom. 8. 32). How thou hast loved us, for whom he who thought it not robbery to be equal with thee became obedient even unto the death of the Cross (Phil. 2. 6), he who alone was free among the dead (Ps. 87. 6), having power to lay down his life and power to take it up again (John 10. 18): for us he was to thee both Victor and Victim, and Victor because Victim: for us he was to thee both Priest and Sacrifice, and Priest because Sacrifice: turning us from slaves into thy sons, by being thy son and becoming a slave. Rightly is my hope strong in him, who sits at thy right hand and intercedes for us (Rom. 8. 34); otherwise I should despair. For many and great are my infirmities, many and great; but thy medicine is of more power. We might well have thought thy Word remote from union with man and so have despaired of ourselves, if it had not been made flesh and dwelt among us.

Terrified by my sins and the mass of my misery, I have pondered in my heart and thought of flight to the desert; but thou didst forbid me and strengthen me, saying: "And Christ died for all: that they also who live, may now not live to themselves but with him who died for them" (2 Cor. 5. 15). See, Lord, I cast my care upon thee, that I may live: and I will consider the wondrous things of thy law (Ps. 118). Thou knowest my unskilfulness and my infirmity: reach me and heal me. He thy only One, in whom are hidden all the treasures of wisdom and knowledge (Col. 2. 3), has redeemed me with his blood. Let not the proud speak evil of me (Ps. 118), for I think upon the price of my redemption, I eat it and drink it and give it to others to eat and drink; and being poor I desire to be filled with it among those that eat and are filled: and they shall praise the Lord that seek him (Ps. 21. 26) (*Confess.*, bk. 10, c. 43. 68, 69, 70).

A few years later, St Augustine returned to the question in his great work on the Trinity. It is the main theme of Book 13, devoted to the restoration of the image of God in man degraded by sin; the price of that recovery shows the greatness of the fault. Theology has drawn much inspiration from these deep and subtle pages in which the holy Doctor defines the meaning and the true demands of justice in this connection, distinguishing them from the somewhat ambiguous formulas of his time.

It is in *The City of God* and in opposing the religious pretensions of the neo-Platonists, particularly of Porphyrus, that St Augustine treated the subject most fully, and we feel when reading it that this is no mere theological treatise; it is a religious way of life that he is defending and that he is anxious to propagate by demonstrating the priesthood of Christ and his sacrifice, which are the main themes of Book 10. The tone of the first pages of this treatise show its profoundly religious character.

In the words of the Greeks, it is to God we owe the worship of latria, in our inward and outward actions; for we are his temple, both as a body and as individuals, and he deigns to take as his dwelling place each member of the faithful as well as the body of the Church, being yet no greater in the whole than in each part of it since his nature is capable neither of extension nor division. When our hearts are lifted up towards him, he is their altar; his only Son is the priest through whom we find favour with him; we sacrifice bloody victims to him when we shed our blood for him or in the cause of truth; the love which consumes us in his presence with a holy and pious flame is the most acceptable incense; we offer to him the gifts he has bestowed upon us, and if we offer ourselves, we give ourselves back to our creator; we call to mind his goodness to us by solemn feasts, lest time should bring ingratitude and forgetfulness; we offer to him on the altar of our hearts aflame with charity, a sacrifice of humility and praise. It is in order to see him, in so far as he can be seen, and to be united to him, that we purify ourselves of the stains of sin and evil passions, and seek to be consecrated in the power of his name; for he is the source of our joy and the object of all our desires. Thus cleaving to him, or rather returning to him instead of separating ourselves from him to our own misfortune, meditating on him and constantly re-reading him (whence, it is said, the origin of the word *religion*), we reach out to him by love, to find rest in him and to possess happiness by possessing perfection. (*City of God*, Bk. 10, c. 3. 2.)

THE CHURCH AND OUR LADY, TEMPLES OF THE HOLY SPIRIT

Christ continues to live, spiritually, in the Church which is his Mystical Body. This doctrine, expressly taught by St Paul (1 Cor. 12. 12–13 and 27), was familiar to the Fathers of the Church. But none of the ancient Doctors developed it with more enthusiasm than St Augustine. One of his basic themes is the comparison of the vine and the branches:

As the body is one and has many members, and as all the members in spite of their number, form a single body, so Christ has many members and a single body. We are all one with Christ our head, we who without a head would have no value. Why? United with our head, we are the vine; separated from him, which God forbid! we would be branches cut off, only fit for the fire. Thus it is said in the Gospel: "I am the vine, you are its branches; my father tends the vine and without me you can do nothing." (John 15. 1, 5.) Lord, if we can do nothing without you we can do everything with you. Indeed, all that he does in us, we appear to do it; but without us he can do much, he can do all things, whereas we can do nothing without him. (*In Ps.* 30: serm. 2, n. 4.)

All the faithful living by the Spirit form a body of which Christ is the head, a city of which he is the leader, a state of which he is King. He is Christ by the royal and priestly unction he has received, and we are so with him by our share in him, we who are his body, for "he makes us one body with him (*concorporans nos sibi*), he makes us his members, so that we should form a single Christ with him. Thus it is that all Christians enjoy that anointing which, in the Old Testament, was reserved to two persons. Hence it follows that we are the body of Christ, since we are all consecrated. In him we are all christs and yet a single Christ, for the head and the members together form the whole Christ. This anointing will bring us to spiritual perfection in the life promised to us." (*In Ps. 26,* serm. 1. 2.)

As Mystical Body, the Church is a living organism, animated by the Holy Spirit given to it at Pentecost, according to our Saviour's promise. Like many other Fathers, St Augustine develops this doctrine which was the mainstay of his great apostolate among the Donatists. While he struggled against the fanatical defenders of the schism, his soul soared in prayerful contemplation of the beauty and grandeur of the Bride of Christ. He often described them in his homilies on the Psalms. In his commentary on Psalm 44, he sings enthusiastically of this mystical union of the Word and the Church.

For St Augustine, devotion to Christ and the Church finds its completion in a true cultus of *Mary,* which is all the more moving since this cultus rose to great heights in the Church only after the definition of the divine motherhood of the Blessed Virgin by the Council of Ephesus, in 431, the year following the holy Doctor's death: he was invited to it but was unable to answer the summons. The cultus of Mary had arisen long before, and the treatises on virginity, which appeared both in the east and in the west in the fourth century, helped to spread it. Its starting-point was the title of "Mother of God", and it met with resistances which were to break up the Council. From the beginning of the fifth century, thirty years before this conflict took place, St Augustine had taken his stand in the early chapters of his treatise "On Virginity", and these pages have a high doctrinal value, not only as regards the question of virginity in general but also as regards the unique status of Mary, the Virgin Mother.

St Augustine goes beyond the subject of the divine maternity, realized in the Incarnation, to proclaim another purely spiritual motherhood of Mary which links her so closely with the Church through which Christians are introduced into the divine life. The Church too is a virgin, spiritually linked with Christ in a virginal marriage; she is also a mother, giving the divine life to men: "Let Christ come to our assistance, the son of the Virgin and the spouse of virgins, born in the flesh of a virgin womb, spiritually betrothed in a virgin marriage. Since, as the Apostle says (2 Cor. 11. 2), the universal Church is a virgin united to a single husband, Christ, of what honour are those of her members not worthy who observe even in their very flesh what she observes altogether in her faith. She takes as her model the mother of her Spouse and Saviour. For the Church too is Mother and Virgin. To whom belongs the integrity over which we keep watch if she is not a Virgin? And whose are the children to whom we are speaking, if she is not Mother?" (*Virg.* 2. 2.)

A fresh parallel, broadly outlined, shows how, in this realm of the spirit, virginity and fertility go hand in hand in Mary and in the Church: "Mary brought into this world, in a bodily manner, the head of this body; the Church brings into the world, after a spiritual manner, the members of this head. In neither case does virginity exclude fertility; in neither case does fertility destroy virginity. Consequently, if the universal Church is holy in body and in spirit, though not all her members are virgin in the bodily sense, but only in spirit, how much holier is she in those of her members in whom she is a virgin both bodily and spiritually!" (*Virg.* 2. 2.)

The general introduction to the treatise continues in the following pages (ch. 4–6), which are specially concerned with the Mother of our Saviour. This teaching of St Augustine on the most holy Virgin must not be separated from another formula of his, the depth of which has not always been appreciated. In his treatise on "Nature and Grace", directed against Pelagius, he declares categorically, after pointing out the universal extent of sin among the descendants of Adam: "We must make an exception, then, in the case of the holy Virgin Mary, for in her case, for the sake of the honour of the Lord, I will not hear of any question of sin of any kind whatsoever" (36, 42; Migne, *P.L.*, 44, col. 267). Clearly the context refers to actual sin. St Augustine does not here deal with the question of original sin; but the formula is so categorical and so all-embracing that we may wonder what he would have answered if the question had been put to him, as it was put to the medieval Doctors. It is not too bold to think that, by a spiritual instinct, as it were, he might have found the reason put forward by Duns Scotus to overcome the objections of those who were rightly anxious to safeguard the truth that we are all saved by Christ.[1] This supposition—only a supposition—becomes all the more plausible when, in accordance with the aim of this book, we study the pervading spiritual tone of the works of the Fathers rather than the technical character of their speculations. These lofty preoccupations were particularly acute in the case of St Augustine, and this at least rids the hypothesis of all improbability.

[1] Mary was preserved from the stain of original sin in view of the merits of Christ.

CHAPTER X

THE IMPORTANCE FOR OUR TIME OF THE ANCIENT MASTERS OF THE CHRISTIAN SPIRIT

The authority of the Fathers as spiritual and mystical guides, as well as teachers of sacred knowledge, has always been recognized by the Church; the teaching value of their writings goes beyond the systematization of doctrine, in spite of a modern tendency to enclose them within those systems. It is most important that we should be aware of possible misconceptions in this respect. Here we shall confine ourselves to pointing out the most obvious which have been made in the history of the Church in the last centuries.

Protestantism, in all the forms it took on in the sixteenth century, appealed to the ancient witnesses of Tradition in order to introduce its innovations into the Church, in contempt of the Church herself, for its greatest mistake was to forget the fundamental rule, laid down by St Irenaeus in the second century, of union with the apostolic See of Rome. This gross fundamental error was accompanied by a number of other deviations in doctrine and in practice which made the Protestant reformation a revolutionary enterprise, first in the religious and then in the social sphere. Reforms were certainly called for, and the Church did carry them out; she was slow in doing so, but she remained faithful to tradition, that is to say to the doctrine of the Fathers and the rules they had elaborated, rendering more explicit for the purposes of applying them, the principles laid down by Christ himself.

Jansenism, which took shape in the eighteenth century, was theoretically much less radical than Protestantism, particularly in its attitude to the Church, whose authority it recognized in principle while actually rejecting it whenever the directives that it received did not coincide with the single rule allowed by its teachers, namely, the authority of St Augustine, to the exclusion of all others. In the last instance, faith in this authority amounted to a blind adherence in dogmatic matters to the authority of the *Augustinus*, a learned work of the future Bishop of Ypres, Cornelius Jansen, otherwise called Jansenius, who was then professor at Louvain and, in the sphere of ethics, to the austere directives given by "Saint Cyran" (Jean Duvergier de Hauranne), and by Arnauld (Antoine), a doctor of the Sorbonne and the youngest of that family who made Port Royal the bulwark of Jansenism in both doctrine and practice. Apart from the fact that St Augustine is not, as they claimed, the sole religious authority of Christian antiquity, his doctrine was narrowly interpreted by the Jansenist clique, and divorced from its true spiritual background in favour of the new intellectual systems. The essence of Christianity is not in a juridical and social system, however necessary this may be; it is not even in a doctrinal code, however great the importance of dogma and ethics; it is in the spiritual life which asserts itself and flourishes within this framework and through these doctrines: in other words, charity, living and lived. Jansenism emphasized the framework to the detriment of the deeper life underlying it, that living faith which, for all the Fathers and especially for St Augustine, was important above all else.

Luther realized this when he appealed to divine inspiration to renew the Christian spirit; but here, as in every other field, he lacked moderation, and his revolt against the Church finally vitiated all that might have been acceptable in his plan of reform. Lutheran mysticism, based primarily on individual inspiration, led to illuminism and greatly aggravated those pseudo-mystical tendencies from which the west suffered at the time of the Reformation, even in Spain.

In the latter case, the excesses were mastered by firm action on the part of the officers of the Inquisition, pontifical and royal, and still more by the providential action of the great Carmelite mystics, St Teresa and St John of the Cross, whose influence spread far and wide. Their work did not stem the tide of Quietism, particularly in France, and its condemnation, though necessary, hindered the development of that true mysticism which was the strength of the ancient Churches, for it was the soul of the primitive Christian communities.

This fact has been clearly shown from various points of view, and it is enough to remind the reader of it. The Fathers' doctrinal method is very different from that of the moderns, even in theology. Aristotelian scholasticism did useful work by emphasizing the philosophical basis of even the loftiest doctrines in the supernatural order. The Renaissance carried on the same tendency by insisting on the natural organization of the sciences. Positive methods were introduced into every field and specialization increased to the great advantage of discovery and research, but not without a certain detriment to men's ability to see life as a whole.

Here, faith is only the basis, a starting-point, essential of course, for nothing can be done without it, but insufficient in itself, for nothing is complete without hope and charity. In a sense, it might even be said that, without these two virtues, nothing is ever truly begun. Faith is only a guide and a starting-point in that quest of the Christian spirit which is the supernatural life in its maturity, if not in its perfection. That was the field in which the ancients excelled and in which they remain unrivalled masters for us. We have set out the elements of their teaching in the various chapters of this book. Here we can confine ourselves to seeking its sources under the guidance of the two greatest teachers of antiquity: St John Chrysostom in the east and St Augustine in the west.

TWO OUTSTANDING MASTERS OF THE CHRISTIAN SPIRIT

St John Chrysostom was a great spiritual director and it is from this viewpoint that we must assess the extent of his influence during his lifetime and still more after his death. He had no love of speculation, which held such attractions for the easterns, especially those who had been conquered by the spirit of neo-Platonism. He regarded philosophy as a vain tissue of words and subtleties. He was not unaware of the rational aspect of Christian teaching; but he sought it only with the dominant intention of showing how faith answers and satisfies the needs of the heart. For him, philosophy is above all a higher form of piety. He differs from other great teachers, who were outstanding in many respects, in that he was first and foremost a spiritual teacher, a zealous apostle and a totally disinterested champion of the claims of truth and morality.

On reading St John Chrysostom we feel that he has a lofty idea of God, of whose attributes he is strongly aware. But he is less concerned with analysing them than with living by them and teaching others to do so. In all his writings he appealed to the power and wisdom of God, his mercy and his love; he proclaimed his justice and his will; he defended his claims most gloriously. Perhaps the finest of his sermons were inspired by the thought of the grandeur of God, and the fragility of creatures, witness his homilies on the fall of Eutropius. His sense of the vanity of the things of this world, so forcefully expressed in them, is based on a clear understanding that God is all: God is the port that knows no storm, the true city, far from which we are but travellers, dwelling in an inn for a day and passing on.

He had been prepared for his mission by an intense spiritual life and, before devoting himself to a life of action, he had been a contemplative in the fullest sense of the word. Thus was engraved for ever in his soul that lofty idea of God which gave unity of purpose to his life and power to his spoken word, guiding him in his extremely practical apostolate, devoted to the defence of morality, as it guides others with different aptitudes or ministerial obligations, in the field of speculative and doctrinal research.

His aim was to make this lofty ideal, glimpsed in solitude, a living reality in the Christian family, by awakening the spirit of prayer. He wished, he said, to transform every Christian household into a "gymnasium of philosophy", because the wife who lives there in peace and quiet can apply herself to prayer, reading and any other "philosophy"—the word being here used to denote a pious exercise. He does not require that we should withdraw into the mountains and deserts to practise it; he wishes to bring it back from the desert to the city, by the practice of virtue and love of the spiritual life. This ideal was later taken up by St Francis de Sales and realized by St Vincent de Paul. The work of these masters must not make us forget the insights of their great precursor.

Much more of a philosopher in the speculative sense, St Augustine was a real thinker, but after the manner of the Fathers, whose thought was never divorced from life, particularly on the supernatural plane. In point of fact, the word which best describes his spiritual character is that of wisdom, the quest for and discovery of God. It has two very different aspects, one purely natural, the other supernatural. St Augustine links them together without confounding them but with a clear emphasis on the second aspect, on which his soul continually dwelt from the time of his conversion, even when dealing with rational truths.

For St Augustine, natural wisdom is merely a rational buttress of Christian wisdom. It is nonetheless real and can lead man to a certain knowledge of God which is the basis of religion and life. In substance, it is a fundamental philosophy, capable of being organized into a system on different levels. God is its centre, and St Augustine lays strong emphasis on this. His philosophy is generally more implicit than clearly formulated. But he explained its basic principles, attributing them to Plato, in that sentence from *The City of God* quoted above (*City of God*, Bk. 8, c. 4 *seq.*). According to this philosopher, he says, God is "both the cause of the existence" of creatures and the "principle of intellection" in all minds, the "rule of life" for all created wills. These words contain a complete doctrine and the nine philosophical dialogues alone contain many explanations of them. But, in spite of its richness, this philosophy remains subordinate to supernatural wisdom.

For St Augustine, the essence of this supernatural wisdom lies in faith, hope and charity. It is essentially a theological wisdom. It is founded on faith, but united to hope and charity, and this is no mere doctrinal union, but a living and progressive one.

In this world, a true cooperation between man and God is necessary for the divine gifts to achieve their full effect. The theological virtues must be continually practised, and this progressive effort is the surest way of achieving that Christian wisdom of which Augustine is the Doctor and the great exponent.

This gradual ascent towards God has many stages and St Augustine described them in various ways. Three of them can serve as a basis for a serious classification, valid for all periods and more necessary than ever in our time. True theological wisdom is found first of all in doctrine and prayer: the first effort on the part of the Christian taught by St Augustine is to cling to the faith in prayer in order to find in it the initial strength required to struggle against evil by observing the commandments. Thus we are well on the way to those heights towards which every Christian is called to strive.

After this first effort, wisdom becomes affective and active, for the initial strength acquired calls forth a greater effort, and love of God lifts the soul towards a more complete self-giving in the service of Christ and souls. In generous souls, it tends to beget a true spirit of conquest and the history of the saints shows its great apostolic achievements.

Without prejudice to this spirit of prayer and action, wisdom, as it approaches perfection, becomes unitive and pacifying. Far from inhibiting action, it often sustains it, but with a strong emphasis on the presence in the soul of the Divine Persons who, under one form or another, show to the faithful soul a friendship bordering on intimacy. In many of St Augustine's works, particularly in the *Confessions,* we find references to these degrees of ascent, especially the third, which comes from union with God. It is surely in the *Confessions* that the Christian of ancient times would have found the clearest and most passionate expression of the union with God. It is through them also that people of our time can enter into closest contact with this great soul and find the Christian spirit best adapted to the contemporary mind, since it derives from the purest sources, those closest to the Gospel.

TRUE SOURCES OF THE CHRISTIAN SPIRIT

We must be very careful here to avoid a danger which threatens even the most Christian of modern thinkers: namely, that of exaggerating the importance of philosophy. Philosophy is necessary, of course, and St Augustine in particular often made use of it; but for the Christian it has a purely auxiliary function. St Augustine had a peculiar grasp of the value of the mind and its activities: this is even his normal way of reaching out to God, with a firmness unsurpassed even by the Aristotelian realism of St Thomas, that inspired adversary of atheistic positivism. St Augustine's spiritual realism, with its latent idealism tempered and completed by the inspiring influence of Plato, corresponds perfectly with that other major tendency of the modern soul. It is of capital importance to make clear the part played by the spirit in man without compromising the essential unity of his nature. The value of the spirit is not purely ideal, and it is because of its profound reality that it provides a sure and rapid way of ascent to God, with a sureness sometimes lacking in the French promoters of the new "Philosophy of the Spirit".

The true philosophy of the spirit is the most direct and perhaps the safest starting-point from which to rise towards the infinite. But it is only a *starting-point* and cannot claim to reach God; he remains transcendent and it is only by a true condescension on his part that man can be united to him by grace. God is Spirit, pure Spirit, and by his very nature he is beyond our reach. Every contingent spirit, inferior to him by nature, is dependent on him in all its supernatural activities which are unthinkable except by a loving condescension on the part of God, the only being who is Pure Spirit and Perfect Spirit, one in nature yet living in Three Persons, as the Christian faith teaches us. In all this, philosophy is completed and enriched in every way by revelation.

The union of man, imperfect spirit, with God who is Pure Spirit, is accomplished, on the one hand, by sanctifying grace, a grace of filial adoption on the part of God, and, on the other hand, by the exercise of the theological virtues, faith, hope and charity, by means of which, in this world already, man can live as a child of God. That is the substance of the Christian spirit, which exists in germ in the baptized child, but which develops only with the cooperation of the adult. It makes itself felt with the awakening of reason, but is refined and perfected only in the years of maturity, in proportion to the generosity and submissiveness of each individual. It has many degrees and can progress by innumerable means.

In the course of this work, we have seen how the Fathers regarded this action of God in humanity and how, thanks to Christ, and above all to the Holy Spirit, humanity has answered its call. These modalities are very varied. Without repeating them in detail we can sum them up by emphasizing the Christian spirit. This includes human reason, but transcends it by divine cooperation. It is not to be confused with the "Holy Spirit", who is a divine Person, transcendent like the Father and the Son, though he assumes in humanity renewed by Christ a lofty mission of inspiration and guidance. The Christian spirit includes both these elements and shows them linked in the baptized soul faithful to grace and generous in the service of God.

The means of strengthening and developing this spirit may have varied in the course of the centuries. It is important to take note of those which best answer the needs of souls at any given time. This work has pointed out particularly those used in Christian antiquity, a period of great spiritual vitality. The scientific culture of the Middle Ages, of the renaissance and of modern times in no way contradicts the value of the patristic period in this respect, and if it has caused it to be forgotten, we must return, by a healthy reaction, to these true sources of the spiritual life in its integrity.

Among many methods, two seem to stand out as being necessary today for the educated Christian, especially for the young, anxious for a deeper Christian life: they are personal prayer and a Christian education of the mind.

Personal prayer is taken here in the fullest sense of the word. All Christian prayer presupposes a certain participation by the person who practises it. Merely to be present in the body is not enough. Attendance at the holiest and most solemn act of worship is not prayer if the person attending it does not have at least the intention of taking part in it with the mind, and still more with the affections. The rites and formulas are merely a preparation or outward condition : prayer implies a certain offering of the heart, however elementary. This spiritual offering can be very intense and effective, in which case attendance at the ceremonies will have great value. Thanks to this inner offering of the soul, prayer can attain a high spiritual level, though rightly called public or common prayer.

There is room beside it for prayer of a mainly personal character; by this is meant that kind of prayer known usually as mental prayer. The main feature of this type of prayer is not the outward ritual nor the recitation of formulas, however devout; it is the *personal offering* of the mind and heart to God, present in the soul by grace, an offering renewed during or after the reading of a passage or the evocation of a memory. St Augustine was a great teacher of this kind of prayer and the most widely read of all the ancient writers, thanks to his *Confessions*.

This work is, in fact, a prolonged mental prayer, in the form of a conversation with God. It did more to spread this practice than the most learned theories, hence the capital importance of St Augustine in the field of personal prayer. He presents it not only in its common form, but, in many pages also, in higher forms in which the action of God is predominant and prayer becomes contemplation. Contemplation, in its turn, intensifies spiritual strength with a view to action and this alone can explain the extraordinary effectiveness and lasting fertility of the main trends of Augustine's teaching, which for centuries were greatly neglected. In our time, the importance of contemplation is being realized once again, without excluding any of those other forms of apostolic activity rendered necessary by modern errors. Contemplation can give life to them all, helping them to recover their deepest vitality, as the Fathers did.

The Christian élites of our time exist partly in the universities; but here a new danger immediately arises, namely that of specialization. This has been made necessary by the abundance of fresh knowledge with its innumerable branches. Specialization is the guarantee of a certain technical value and serious depth of study. But we must try to keep the balance and remember particularly that certain elements of higher culture are universally required and even if there is specialization in this field too, it contains basic elements of universal application which must be made clear from the beginning. This is indeed the case with the observations of the "spirit" condensed in the preceding pages on the Christian Spirit, observations which presuppose some notions about "spirit" in general and clear principles touching the only being who is Pure Spirit, namely God. These themes appear elementary, but in fact they are the starting-point in every line of thought, human or Christian. Hence the necessity for a real Christian education of the spirit which must in fact be a Christian education by the Spirit. Nothing could be more important as a preliminary to university studies in our time.

This higher specialization is aimed precisely at combating the effects of current specialization, by emphasizing from the start the importance of the truths of the faith and their demands, and by emphasizing, too, the capital importance of the Fathers who were less scholars in the usual sense than "spiritual writers and mystics". The Fathers, like the inspired writers themselves, played a great part in leading Christians to a higher culture of the spirit, even the most specialized.

GENERAL LIST OF THE MOST IMPORTANT FATHERS

A. THE INITIATORS: FIRST THREE CENTURIES

I. *The Apostolic Fathers*

St Clement of Rome (†c. 100)
St Ignatius of Antioch (†c. 106)
St Polycarp (†c. 156)

Hermas (wrote under Pius I, c. 150)
Didache (end of 2nd century)
Various other anonymous writers (2nd century)

II. *Apologists and controversialists*

St Justin (†166)
St Theophilus of Antioch (end of 2nd century)
St Irenaeus (†c. 201)

Minucius (end 2nd century)
Tertullian (end 2nd–beginning 3rd century)
St Victor of Rome (Pope 188–199)

III. *Forerunners of the Great Century*

Clement of Alexandria (end 2nd–beginning 3rd century)
St Hippolytus (†c. 235)
Origen (†c. 254)
Dionysius of Alexandria (†c. 265)
St Cyprian (†258)

Novatian (†258)
Arnobius the Elder (†327)
Lactantius (†325)
St Reticius (†beginning 4th century)
St Lucianus of Antioch (†312)
St Methodius of Olympus (†311)

B. THE GREAT CENTURY: THE GREAT CHRISTIAN THINKERS: 313–461

I. *The Nicaeans*

St Athanasius (295–375)
St Hilary of Poitiers (315–67)
Eusebius of Caesarea (265–340)
St Cyril of Jerusalem (313–86)
St Epiphanius (315–403)
Didymus the Blind (313–98)

St Ephrem the Syrian (306–73)
St Aphraates (c. 345)
St Basil the Great (330–79)
St Gregory Nazianzen (330–89 or 90)
St Gregory of Nyssa (335–c. 95)

II. *Great Exegetes and Spiritual Writers*

Diodorus (330–94)

Theodore of Mopsuestia (350–428)

St John Chrysostom (345–407)

Palladius (363–425)

St Antony (*c.* 250–356)

Cassian (*c.* 360–435)

St Damasus (Pope 366–84)

St Innocent I (Pope 409–17)

St Ambrose (333–97)

St Paulinus (348–431)

Prudentius (348–*c.* 405)

Rufinus (345–411)

St Jerome (347–419)

St Optatus (4th century)

St Augustine (354–430)

III. *First Doctors of the Incarnation*

St Cyril of Alexandria (375–444)

Theodoret of Cyrus (395–458)

Rabulas of Edessa (†436)

Sahak III the Armenian (†440)

Diadochus of Photike (mid 5th century)

St Leo the Great (Pope 440–61)

St Peter Chrysologus (406–50)

St Maximus of Turin (mid 5th century)

Salvianus (5th century; †*c.* 480)

St Hilary of Arles (†449)

St Vincent of Lérins (†450)

Claudianus Mamertus (†474)

Julian Pomerus (†498)

St Prosper (†*c.* 463)

C. THE CONTINUATORS: END OF THE PATRISTIC PERIOD: 461–843

I. *In the West*

St Gelasius (Pope 492–6)

St Ennodius (473–521)

Faustus of Riez (5th century)

St Gregory of Tours (5th century)

St Fulgentius (*c.* 648–533)

St Avitus (†519)

St Sidonius (431–89)

St Caesarius of Arles (470–543)

St Fortunatus (530–600)

Boethius (470–525)

Cassiodorus (477–570)

St Benedict (480–*c.* 543 or 553)

St Gregory the Great (Pope 590–604)

St Isidore of Seville (†636)

St Columbanus (540–615)

St Bede the Venerable (†735)

II. *In the East*

Leontius of Byzantium (†542)

Justinian (Emperor 527–65)

"Dionysius the Areopagite" (end of 5th century)

St John Climacus (6th–7th century)

St Romanus (6th–7th century)

St Sophronius (550–638)

St Maximus (580–662)

St Germanus (635–733)

St Andrew of Crete (660–740)

St John Damascene (*c.* 675–749)

St Theodore the Studite (759–836)

SELECT BIBLIOGRAPHY

CAYRÉ, F.: *A Manual of Patrology and the History of Theology*, Paris, Desclée, 1956. (This book contains full bibliographies for each chapter.)

LEBRETON, J., and ZEILLER, J.: *The History of the Primitive Church* (translated by Ernest C. Messenger, four volumes), London, Burns Oates, 1942–8, New York, Macmillan.

HOARE, L.: *The Western Fathers* (the lives of SS Martin, Augustine, Honoratus, Germanus and Ambrose), London and New York, Sheed and Ward, 1954.

DE LUBAC, H., S.J.: *Catholicism*, London, Burns Oates, and New York, Longmans, 1950.

PRZYWARA, E.: *An Augustine Synthesis,* London and New York, Sheed and Ward, 1945.

The Confessions of St Augustine. There are many translations of which the most recent is that by F. J. Sheed, London and New York, Sheed and Ward, 1951.

POURRAT, P.: *Christian Spirituality*, volumes I–III, London, Burns Oates, 1922–4, and Westminster, Maryland, Newman Press, volumes I–IV, 1953–5.

QUASTEN, JOHANNES, and PLUMPE, JOSEPH C., Editors, *Ancient Christian Writers*. The Works of the Fathers in translation. A series of translations into English of which to date some thirty volumes have appeared. Westminster, Maryland, Newman Press and London, Longmans 1946–.